Covid Crisis
101 Unanswered Questions

Hugh Williams

St Edward's Press Ltd

Covid Crisis – 101 Unanswered Questions

<u>Formal notes</u>

First published in 2021 by

St Edward's Press Ltd

Registered Office and trading address

20 Barra Close

Highworth

Swindon

Wilts, SN67HX

01793 762417

info@stedwardspress.co.uk

www.stedwardspress.co.uk

For orders and administrative office please contact the publisher at the above address

© St Edward's Press Ltd

ISBN: 978-1-909650-21-3

Cover design by 659design, Highworth
Printed by Ashford Ltd, Gosport.

Covid Crisis – 101 Unanswered Questions

Contents

"A contempt for real knowledge is fundamentally unchristian; not so a distrust of many of our modern academic processes."

Dom Aelred Graham *The Love of God*

"If a layman suspects that something wrong is going on, then, by use of his reason, he can, and should, warn others about such dangers. When he gives such a warning, he simply serves as a watchdog who gives the alarm."

Dr. Don Felix Sarda Y Salvany's *What is Liberalism?*

To which might be added this quote from an unnamed Spanish Bishop

"It behooves watchdogs to bark."

"If a law is unjust, a man is not only right to disobey it, he is obligated to do so"

Thomas Jefferson

Covid Crisis
101 Unanswered Questions

Foreword
by
Michael Morley

Many people during this last year have had the uneasy feeling that we are not being told the full story of the current Covid-19 pandemic which has seen, with one or two exceptions, the whole world locked down with negative consequences as a result. The actions taken by governments across the globe to eradicate this virus seem to have brought about more distress upon humanity than confidence that the correct actions are being taken.

Considering all the negative evidence that has been accruing during the pandemic, Hugh Williams, among many others, has been disturbed that the mainstream media has not been asking the right questions regarding the harmful side-effects of the global response which have become more obvious and more dire as time has elapsed. As an author, he has decided to ask some of those questions himself and this book is the result.

It has been my privilege as Hugh's friend and colleague, to have been asked to lend some advice and, at one point during our discussions he confessed that as a non-medic he was concerned that he had no qualifications to put pen to paper on this subject. I think I was able to put his mind at rest by reminding him that, as a potential Covid patient himself, he has every right to ask each of the one hundred and one questions that this book raises, especially since, to this date, they have never been answered. And, it would appear, deliberately not answered.

As for Hugh's lack of medical qualifications, he is on common ground with Bill Gates: The same Bill Gates who, with no medical qualifications whatever, but with highly questionable motives and extraordinary audacity, presumes to spearhead the global reaction to Covid and the drive to vaccinate everyone on earth! It might also be of interest to point out here that Matt Hancock, although serving as British Secretary of State for Health and Social Care is similarly not blessed with any medical qualification!

So therefore, Hugh, have no qualms; in the words of the great Duke of Wellington: "Publish and be damned!"

Michael Morley

Preface

What this booklet is all about

Each of us has to decide the truth about the Covid crisis. We can all readily accept that it can often be a very nasty disease, which sometimes leads to the death of the patient. That is undeniably true.

But how about the rest of what we are told about Covid-19?

- Is it <u>naturally</u> occurring?
- Is it <u>highly</u> contagious?
- Is the death rate from it so high that we need to <u>destroy our economy</u> in order to manage the disease?
- Is it really so dangerous that we need to shut down the world, <u>forcing everyone to stay indoors and wear masks when shopping</u> and at school?
- Is it also so dangerous that <u>we must all be given a vaccine</u>, and is the vaccine <u>safe</u>?

If one reads the press and watches the television one would think that the answer to each of the above questions is clearly "Yes." On the other hand, there are thousands of doctors and medical specialists around the world who are speaking out and saying that the answer to each of these five questions is a resounding "No!". The problem being that these dissenting voices have been stifled.

This means that, since one is unlikely to find any reports of what these dissenting voices say in the mainstream media, one needs to search extremely hard to discover what these brave professionals are warning us about. If one should happen to notice a report about these opposite views in the mainstream media, it seems that it will invariably be accompanied by negativity and often sneering hostility. What is worse is that this sort of contemptuous propaganda for any alternative explanation of what is actually going on, has been willingly adopted by millions of people in this country, including our nearest and dearest; and this to the effect that they will not be at all interested in the answers to these questions. Their minds have been is made up – or, rather, have been made up for them.

An additional and important question is, "Does not this blanket ban on publishing dissent from the official Covid narrative make one very suspicious?"

The banning of any contrary narrative means that one needs to be pretty resolute if one is to keep an open mind as one searches for the truth. Resolute in terms of research and resolute and prudent in how one talks about such matters with one's friends and family

The author of this booklet believes that the simplest way to decide who is telling the truth, is to ask simple and straightforward questions that challenge the five basic questions above.

If one does this, and reads what the other side has to say and then finds that these important questions have never been answered, let alone properly addressed by officialdom, the nature of the questions themselves and especially the way that they have been ignored, will provide us with a host of intriguing and straightforward answers that we have been deliberately denied.

Before we close this preface, perhaps it would be as well to recall that, when faced with a frightening dilemma such as this, the most reliable way of working out who is telling the truth is to apply that famous Biblical maxim of, "By their fruits ye shall know them."

Hugh Williams
April 2021

The Covid Crisis – 101 Unanswered Questions

We have already said that we believe that the most sensible way to decide who is telling the truth about this grave crisis, is to ask simple and straightforward questions in connection with the five fundamental questions that were raised in the Preface.

Of course, this book is dealing with an ongoing crisis and so, while apologising for saying so, it is highly likely that the following list of questions will neither be comprehensive nor up to date. Nonetheless, let us begin:

1   Is the virus <u>naturally</u> occurring?

1. If it were naturally occurring then, surely, there is no way that we would know in advance when it might appear? So, how come Dr Fauci, the Director of the US National Institute of Allergy and Infectious Diseases (NIAID), when talking about infectious diseases in 2017, announced, "In the next two years there will be a surprise outbreak. There is no doubt in anyone's mind about this."?

2. One wonders why it would be a *surprise* if he *already knew* it was going to happen?

3. How come Sir Richard Dearlove, former head of MI6, said in June 2020 that he had seen an "important" new scientific report by a Norwegian / British Research team suggesting the virus did not emerge naturally but was man-made by Chinese scientists?

4. *The Daily Telegraph*, concluded in the summer of 2020 that this coronavirus should correctly be called "Wuhan virus" and claimed to have proven "beyond reasonable doubt that the Covid-19 virus is engineered". Why has so little attention been paid to this startling announcement?

5. Why are numerous doctors saying that the virus was manipulated in the laboratory prior to being released?

6.   With this virus originating in China, why has that country not allowed any sort of proper investigation into the outbreak?

7.   And why has China punished Australia for daring to ask for such an investigation?

8.   Why have official camera crews from abroad not been allowed anywhere near the Wuhan laboratory?

9.   In maintaining that Coronavirus is not a naturally occurring virus, Dr Judy Mikovits, who has worked closely with Dr Fauci, is convinced that this strain of Coronavirus (known as SARS Covid 2 Virus) was manipulated in the laboratory. It might have occurred naturally after, say, eight hundred years of natural development, but to have appeared within ten years proves that it was deliberately manipulated. Should we not take notice of her conviction?

10. Dr Mikovits does not know if the release of the virus was deliberate. In her professional opinion, it was released by either the laboratory at Fort Detrick in Maryland, where she worked in 1999, or the Wuhan laboratory. Should we not be told more about the origin of this disease?

11. Before we leave Dr Fauci, with him apparently masterminding the US's reaction to Covid, why does he refuse to be tested for Covid? He was heard to say this on an interview at a press conference that was seen in early April 2021.

2   Is the virus <u>highly</u> contagious?

12. According to a group of Polish doctors who spoke out about what is happening in the autumn of 2020, the spread of the virus occurs through droplet infection (only in patients who cough or sneeze) and aerosol spray in closed, unventilated rooms. Therefore contamination is impossible in the open air. So why have people not been allowed to enjoy the outside and

why, for instance, can two people go for a walk together but they may not play golf or other outdoor sports?

13. Again according to the Polish doctors, contact tracing and epidemiological studies show that healthy people (or asymptomatic carriers with a positive test result) are almost incapable of transmitting the virus, hence they are not a threat to each other. So, why have such people been forced to lockdown? You can read more about these Polish doctors in Appendix One.

14. The transmission of the virus by handling money or touching a shopping trolley has not been scientifically proven. So, why the ubiquitous signs asking us to pay only by card?

3 Is the death rate from it so high that we need to <u>destroy our economy</u> in order to manage the disease?

15. According to government figures, the deaths from Covid by mid-March 2021 numbered 125,000. Putting to one side the fact that, as you are about to read, many deaths have been recorded as having been due to Covid when such was clearly *not* the case, which means that the Covid deaths have been significantly overstated, 125,000 out of a UK population of 67,000,000, means that just 0.0187% of the population, or 1 in over 500 people. Please remember that fraction of 1 death in 500 of the UK's population.

    Put that against either the Black Death (1348) or the Great Plague (1665) and while estimates may vary, at least 1 in 5 of the population died during those plagues. 1 in 5, please note which is a million miles away from Covid's score of 1 in 500. Why have we locked down and destroyed our economy for such a low death rate?

16. In a recent press article, one sufferer said "Everyone in Spain knows someone that's lost someone to Covid." This statement *sounds* a horrendous statistic (something to put the fear of God into you), until, when you look at it again, you realise that it's actually an unremarkable statistic and not unlike the situation in the UK. Putting it another way, most people

do not know anyone who has died, but they probably know someone who does know someone who has died.

If, for sake of argument, each of us knows 250 people, then since I know 250 people and one of those people knows a different 250, and between our 500 acquaintances, one has died with, or of Covid, that more or less supports the fact that just 1 in 500 have died of Covid at the time of writing.

In the author's case and at the time of writing, he knows of just one person who has died and whose death was registered as due to Covid. But only one, and the sufferer was elderly and infirm (he had nearly died about ten years previously) and so such a death should really have been described as "with Covid" and not "of Covid." Can you see how the mainstream media casually drops a statement like the statement quoted in the first line of this point to mislead the unwary that the deaths are far more prevalent than is actually the case?

17. How about this letter to the *Daily Telegraph* on 10th February 2021?

Certified Covid deaths

SIR – My 94-year-old cousin died recently. Despite her having no symptoms, and negative Covid testing, her GP put Covid on the death certificate, even though he had not been to see her. At the family's insistence, that untruth was removed, and a more honest cause added. The GP rang to apologise.

How many more of these false certificates are being signed and what effect are they having on statistics?

Peter Welsh, Sale, Cheshire

The author has also heard of several similar disgraceful incidents involving the deliberately misleading reports on death certificates. For a professional doctor deliberately to misreport a death as Covid when it was clearly not, and especially when he had not even seen the deceased, and even more especially since the government stopped all autopsies at the beginning of this so-called pandemic, seems to many, to be nothing short of criminal. Should not he and his like be struck off?

The *Daily Telegraph* has published at least one other similar letter since the start of the Covid Crisis.

18. It is important also to recall that the deaths from Covid are a fraction of the grim forecasts on which the lockdown regulations, and the associated fines for not obeying them, have been based. Why does the government never admit that it got it wrong and that there is no reason at all for controlling everyone's movements?

19. The reason the government got it so wrong would appear to be that, in the spring of 2020, it took the advice of Professor Neil Ferguson of Imperial College London, that in a worst case scenario, half a million people might die of Covid. They had taken his advice on similar diseases over the previous twenty years in which he warned that worst case scenarios of:

   - Foot and Mouth 2001, might result in 150,000 deaths. Fewer than 200 died but millions of animals were slaughtered.
   - BSE, 2000 might result in 50,000 deaths. 177 people died.
   - Bird Flu 2005. Warning 150,000 deaths. 282 people died.
   - Swine Flu 2009. Warning 65,000 deaths. 457 died.

   With such a questionable record, why does the government appoint such a man and such an institution to advise it?

20. To make matters worse Professor Ferguson, having advised the government to institute a strict lockdown, was then caught breaking his own rules by meeting his mistress. So, again, why, in 2021, is such a man still advising the government?

21. Even the press has reported that 95% of the supposed Covid fatalities actually had underlying causes. So why does the government keep pumping out the fake propaganda that makes us think that over 100,000 people have

died *from* Covid – *not with* Covid – thus frightening the whole population into thinking that everyone is going to die?

22. How come large groups of doctors in Germany, Belgium, Spain, the USA and elsewhere have spoken out openly against what is happening? 500 doctors in Germany and 600 in Spain have described the pandemic as "planned" and 1,400 doctors in Belgium, when talking about the measures being taken to combat this disease, say "There is no longer any medical justification for this (lockdown) policy." Their views have been famously supported by those who have drawn up the Great Barrington Declaration and the thousands who have added their signatures to it. And this at a time when the tests are giving a frightening number of false-positive results. In one instance this has been calculated as being about 90% false positives. Why do governments invariably both sneer at, as well as disdainfully ignore, such expert opinion?

23. The Belgian doctors have gone on to say that the public communication about this by the news media has been more like propaganda than objective reporting. Having watched and listened to hundreds of news broadcasts that never question the effectiveness of Lockdown, am I allowed to wonder if misleading the public over such an important matter has been deliberate?

24. Why have a number of such medical specialists, who have questioned what is going on, been silenced; some even losing their licences to practise?

25. With there being so relatively few deaths (one in about 500 in the UK, and this figure includes many instances of deaths reported as having been due to Coronavirus when such was blatantly *not* the case), and with 97% of those who catch it recovering, why are whole economies throughout the world being destroyed on the back of a disease that is affecting so relatively few people?

26. Does it not look as if we have destroyed our economy, needlessly? Or might one even say that it has been done deliberately, since the UK government has refused MPs any vote to challenge its decision?

27. Why are the authorities openly admitting that they are taking a very liberal approach by deliberately describing a significant number of deaths as Covid-related when this has clearly not been the case?

28. Why have death certificates been signed with so little double checking?

29. Why have doctors in the USA been rewarded with extra funding ($13,000) for reporting a death as having been caused by Coronavirus?

30. Furthermore, if such inducements to misreport deaths have happened in the United States and if there have clearly been cases of misreporting of deaths in the UK, is this because doctors in the UK have also been rewarded with inducements for reporting a death as having been caused by Covid-19 when this has definitely not been the case?

31. Added to which, why have doctors been given three times as much ($39,000) for putting patients on a ventilator, especially when ventilators are more likely to cause long-term lung damage, and indeed more likely to kill the patient, than if he or she is not put on a ventilator?

32. Here is what Mike Adams of *Natural News* has to say about ventilators: The Use of Ventilators – A short talk by Mike Adams of Natural News. http://www.thetruthseeker.co.uk/?p=207715
"Covid is not a viral pneumonia but a condition of oxygen deprivation. People are dying from lack of oxygen. This is why they are put onto ventilators but ventilators force pressure into the lungs, thereby damaging the delicate membrane in the lungs. This means that if the patient survives he or she will have permanently damaged lungs, as I know from my knowledge of two such people who were treated in this way, one of whom has died."

Is not the use of ventilators on such patients an outrage?

33. And then there is this shocking story from a retired surgeon who does not want to be named:

    "Johnson's boast of 31,500 mechanical ventilators (for Covid patients) is not only medically illiterate, it is potentially lethal on a large scale. This is something of which I have had first-hand experience as a cardiac surgeon. Mechanical ventilators, even in young patients with healthy lungs, can be more dangerous than the open-heart surgery which necessitated their use. I would estimate in my day more than half of our post-operative deaths at the National Heart Hospital were due to mechanical ventilation (VDs). Of course, this did not appear on the death certificates. Even today the use of mechanical ventilation in patients with lung infections is highly controversial (Think about it - pumping oxygen under pressure into fragile damaged lungs - of course they burst). Fatality rates are around eighty to ninety percent even when managed by highly specialised teams of ICU staff twenty-four hours a day.

    "Earlier this year my daughter worked as a staff nurse on an Acute Care Covid ward at Kings College Hospital where ventilators were being used. She begged to be transferred to any other ward because she could not bear witnessing and being compelled to assist in the killing of elderly patients by putting them on ventilators when everyone knew that it would kill them. And it did - it burst their lungs. In the end, my daughter, a born-again believer, after telling me on the phone from the hospital: "It's evil, Dad, it's evil," attempted to commit suicide. She has still not recovered - barring a miracle she never will.

    "The 'Nightingale Hospitals' with hundreds of ICU beds with ventilators are killing sheds."

    Are we really meant to ignore such dissident voices and keep swallowing the propaganda that the mainstream media keep shovelling our way to keep us both quiet and frightened?

8

3.a. Lockdowns

34. And it is not as if lockdowns have led to lower mortality. Thanks to Nick Kollerstrom, take these figures from https://www.worldometers.info/coronavirus/country/ and count up to March 1st. They compare deaths in countries that have locked down with those that have not applied such stringent controls:

High Lockdown			
Country	'CV deaths'	Population in millions	Deaths per million
UK	123,125	66.5	1851
USA	527,394	328	1607
France	86,890	67.0	1296
Italy	97,945	60.3	1624
Spain	69,609	46.9	1484
Mean:			1572 ± 203

Low Lockdown			
Country	'CV deaths'	Population in millions	Deaths per million
Sweden	13,021	10.2	1276
Japan	7,887	126	62
Belarus	1,986	9.5	209
Nicaragua	173	6.5	26
Mean:			239 ± 593

So why do the UK authorities keeping insisting on imposing such severe lockdowns when they are clearly ineffective?

35. How about this letter published by the *Daily Telegraph* on 17th March 2021:

   Lockdowns don't work

   SIR – The suggestion that "it's unarguable that we should have gone into lockdown earlier" is simply wrong.

   The weight of academic evidence is that lockdowns have little independent impact on hospitalisations and deaths. In contrast, voluntary changes to behaviour seem to be a significant factor in slowing and eventually reversing surges in infections.

   Given the lag between infection and death, the fact that Covid-related deaths peaked in England on April 8 last year suggests that infections had begun to drop well before the national lockdown on March 23. More recently, every indicator confirms that infections were falling in England well before the third national lockdown in January.

   What is certain, however, is that compulsory lockdown restrictions have carried unimaginable economic and social costs to society – to say nothing of their devastating impact on freedom, basic rights and respect for the law.

   Professor David Paton, and a number of other professionals.

   Why does the government deliberately ignore such wise commentators?

36. Why, in the light of this horrendous situation, has the UK government refused to carry out a cost / benefit analysis of the effect of the lockdown?

37. Even the World Health Organisation has said that lockdowns cause huge damage. Why has our government paid no attention to their advice over this?

4 Is it really so dangerous that we need to shut down the world, <u>forcing everyone to stay indoors and wear masks when shopping</u> and at school?

4.a Masks

38. Let us start with this brilliant article in the *Daily Telegraph* by a teenager, Mac Morton, dated 9th March 2021:

I'm 15. Don't you dare tell me that masks in school are harmless

"I was desperate to get back to school. But masks have ruined it.

"This might not be something you often hear teenagers say, but I've been desperate to get back to school ever since it shut. So you'd think I'd have got what I wanted now. But I haven't. When I said I wanted to go back to school, I was assuming I'd be able to breathe freely.

"Children and teenagers have sacrificed a lot over the last six months. We've missed our friends, our hobbies, our work and much more. Of course to an extent, that's true for everyone. But missing out on these things is a lot harder for teenagers than for adults: we're at that stage of our life where we grow away from our families and towards our friends, so they are our priority. Being away from them has been the equivalent of an adult being forced away from the family they've created. What makes it even harder to take is everyone telling us that not only is it wrong to meet our friends, but it's selfish simply to want the things we've lost back – or even to be upset at not having them.

"I don't know about other people, but my friends and I didn't even say goodbye before lockdown. We didn't want to. What do you even say when you don't know when you'll next see someone? Where do you start? "And I didn't want to say goodbye, because that made it too real. I felt like it wouldn't be so hard if I refused to turn my back on the things that were about to go. But it made no difference – it's impossible not to feel the loss. Teenage friendship isn't something that can just be put in a box and ignored, even for a short time.

"And now we're back in the classroom, things are hardly any better. People view masks as a fairly minor restriction, with minor impacts. That's not true.

"As Molly Kingsley pointed out in The *Telegraph*, in Germany a study of over 25,000 children wearing masks throughout the school day reports headaches (53%), difficulty concentrating (50%), malaise (42%), impaired learning (38%) and drowsiness or fatigue (37%); in France social media is awash with reports of parents measuring children's oxygen levels at the end of the school day and finding them to be dangerously low.

"That all chimes with my own personal experience. After the second lockdown, I went to a meeting with a youth club where we all wore masks. It was downright miserable: no one spoke, personalities seemed blunted. Then they sent us outside for a break, and instantly everyone went back to their normal selves. But the second we went in and put the masks back on, everyone disappeared behind them again.

"The only reason I was at that youth group was to see my friends, but I stopped going after that, because it wasn't worth seeing the masked version of them.

"People my age want to be in school primarily for the social element. Masks remove that. We're all just exhausted by sadness and anger, desperate to escape or even just to breathe for a minute, because we've had no break since March 2020.

"Now that Covid cases are plummeting by the day and an effective vaccine has been offered to all vulnerable groups, isn't it time to give teenagers like me our lives back?"

Isn't it an utter disgrace that our pusillanimous government has paid not the slightest attention to the plight of youngsters like Mac Morton?

39. The use of masks has become obligatory on the understanding that they reduce the risk of droplet infection. However, the weave of the cotton masks has a size of the order of micrometres, whereas the size of the virus is one thousand times smaller, which clearly means that masks do not stop viruses passing through them. With no physical grounds to claim that masks protect the wearer against airborne viruses, nor likewise do they reduce the risk for others when the wearer releases the virus, what is the point of wearing masks?

40. The wearing of masks has side-effects.
     i.   Oxygen deficiency occurs fairly quickly and has an effect similar to altitude sickness; which results in headache, nausea, fatigue, loss of concentration etc.,
     ii. Patients also complain of sinus and breathing problems.
     iii. Accumulated CO_2 leads to toxic acidification of the body, which adversely affects immunity.
     iv. A room or workplace should contain no more than the standard 900 parts per million of CO_2, with a maximum of 1,200 in certain circumstances; but after wearing a mask for a minute this toxic limit is significantly elevated to three to four times these limits. It is like breathing in a poorly ventilated room.
     v.   The mask covers a large part of the face, making it impossible to recognise, interpret or imitate facial expressions. Facial expressions are one of the most important aspects of interpersonal communications.

Have these points ever been raised in the press or the media?

41. An area of the brain, known as the FFA (facial fusion area) matures in development age. If a face is covered with a mask most of the time during this phase of development (such as hours spent in school) there is a risk that the area may disappear, making the child no longer able to distinguish one face from another. Under these circumstances there is a risk that the child will grow up asexually.

As with other points in this book, why is this fact never addressed by the government?

42. All of which puts a big question over the strategy of social isolation and mandatory wearing of masks for healthy people. There is no scientific evidence to back up this requirement. So why are we forced to wear masks?

4.b Social Distancing
43. Why are doctors saying that social distancing, rather than reducing the chances of this disease spreading, by minimising human contact and the

body's natural ability to build up resistance to these infections, actually reduces the body's ability to fight disease?

44. With peaceful anti-lockdown demonstrations broken up by the police on the grounds that they broke social-distancing rules, but violent Black Lives Matter demonstrations allowed to continue while the police merely watched from the sides, don't we have to ask why the enforcement of the social-distancing regulations have been so perplexingly inconsistent?

45. Doctors have said that closing the beaches and open spaces is a criminal thing to do. It is at such places that one meets with other microbes in the sand, water and in the air – microbes that boost our immune system. Why have we been denied access to such obviously healthy places?

46. Why are local authorities not allowed to determine whether a lockdown is required in their area?

47. The Irish government have decreed that, while the Coronavirus crisis lasts, attending Mass is now illegal. In a newspaper report of March 28th 2021 (Passion Week) shocking images emerged of the Gardai taking the names of Catholics in Limerick while they prayed outside the Sacred Heart Church.

As has been intimated in the Preface to this book, namely that we should judge this situation on the basis of "By their fruits ye shall know them.", are we not entitled to think that, if Catholics are not allowed to pray in the open, and churches elsewhere have been ordered shut, Satan, himself is now in charge of world events?

4.c The Mild Acceptance of these Restrictions by the Public

48. Is it not extraordinary how willingly shops, businesses and people in general have mildly accepted and imposed the need for social distancing?

49. Is it not truly frightening how most of the population have accepted these restrictions not only without questioning but, in a number cases, with hostility towards those who, for example, do not wear masks?

50. There have been a number of stories like this but this is one that has been verified by the author: Someone near Oxford organised a dinner party during lockdown for ten people, which was illegal. All ten guests duly attended which led to a neighbour noticing the cars parked outside the house concerned. The neighbour then phoned the police and told them what appeared to be happening; the police duly turned up and imposed a £10,000 fine. Would you welcome neighbours like this?

51. Here is an extract of a paper written in January 2021 by Tom Hodgkinson, the founder of the Idler Academy and editor of *The Idler* Magazine:

"In E.M. Forster's *The Machine Stops* shopping is a thing of the past. The citizenry live in luxurious little cells and have everything they want – food, entertainment, medicine – delivered to them via tubes. They are physically weak and indeed strong-looking babies are put to death. The people communicate via iPad type devices and rarely leave their rooms. When they do leave, they summon airships which arrive at their door in the manner of an Uber. They have thousands of online friends and spend their time attending or delivering lectures. The story was written in 1909.

"In Huxley's *Brave New World* from 1932, books have been banned in the manner of Plato's *Republic*. No one is allowed to read Shakespeare as it might make them ask questions. Freedom has been sacrificed for comfort, and the inhabitants are made very comfortable indeed: they have non-stop sex and when things get rough they bliss out on the drug Soma, a sort of cross between Prozac and Ecstasy. The great achievement of the authorities, says Huxley, is to have created a situation where the people love their slavery. "Everybody's happy nowadays," says one character, in a phrase later to be made into an excellent pop-punk tune by The Buzzcocks.

"In Orwell's *Nineteen-Eighty-Four*, written in 1948, giant screens dominate the sitting room. These screens watch you while you watch them. They know what you are doing. Google, Facebook, YouTube and the government are thrown into one entity called Big Brother. The people are kept in a state of constant anxiety: the country is perpetually terrorized by an ever-changing threat. They're allowed to express their rage in a weekly session called Two Minutes Hate where they scream and shout at enemies on a big screen. In each of these stories, we follow the progress of a rebel, one Nietzschean individual who makes an heroic effort to smash the system, but fails tragically.

"The parallels with our time are plain to see. We are encouraged to live in a state of fear and to value security over really being alive. Our every move is tracked and traced and online search engines know our deepest and darkest thoughts, desires and fears. For decades we've been locked in an ever-changing crisis: Suez crisis, three day week, war on the unions, Falklands war, war on Iraq, war on terror, war on drugs, war on EU, civil war over Brexit, war on Covid. A fearful, anxious and cowed populace is easier to control and insecure citizens tend to make excellent consumers. And as Jaron Lanier has argued, a desire to control is at the heart of the Internet: computer networks were conceived with Skinner's behaviourism in mind. They're all about behaviour modification. The goal is a population which does what it's told.

"Western governments are looking at China with something that looks a little like envy: how obedient, docile and eager to please their population is! How civic-minded! And how successful! Both left and right, at a certain level, are internally rejoicing over the expanding power of states and the extent of their own empires."

Were these writers deluded in their imaginings or were they uncannily accurate in what they foresaw?

52. And what of the fines and prison sentences that have been introduced? You can be given a £10,000 fine for organising a demonstration against the government's policy to manage Covid.
Or fined £5,000 for going abroad without permission.

And when you return from abroad you might find yourself imprisoned for up to 10 years.

Are we governed by a bunch of sadists?

53. And how about these two images?

Big Brother 1984: This is taken from the film 1984, which was, of course, based on George Orwell's book with the same title.

Big Brother 2020 the UK Health Secretary, Matt Hancock M.P., in the spring of 2020. Is this comparison fair? Was the 2020 scene set up deliberately to scare us?

5 Is it also so dangerous that <u>we must all be given a vaccine and is the vaccine safe</u>?

54. Why is there so much emphasis on the need for compulsory vaccination to combat this disease when numerous medics say that such injections for this disease will put human life in danger, as they have in the past? (One thinks of the swine flu vaccines having to be destroyed after it was shown that they left certain children permanently disabled.)

55. And why have the drug companies that produce the vaccine been given immunity from prosecution? Indeed why have some life assurance companies announced that they may not pay out for deaths caused by the vaccine?

56. And why was this immunity given at a time when the vaccines were being launched and long before any long-term side-effects could possibly be known?

Have we learned no lessons since the tragedy of Thalidomide? An infamous case where too little research was done on a drug before reaching the market in the early 1960s with the claim that it was completely safe and could be taken as a tranquilliser even by pregnant women; only for many babies to be born with deformed limbs. With this disaster in mind, can we be sure that enough research has been done on the novel anti-Covid vaccines during the few short months before they began to be injected into millions of rather less than well-informed people with no symptoms?

57. And coupled with this question, why has the BBC said that it will not interview anyone who is against the Covid vaccination?

58. Why is Bill Gates, with no medical qualifications, calling for the whole world to be vaccinated? The answer may lie in the final sentence of this article by Peter Koenig of Global Research dated March 2nd 2021…

"For over twenty years Bill Gates and his Foundation, the Bill and Melinda Gates Foundation (BMGF) have been vaccinating foremost children by the millions in remote areas of poor countries, mostly Africa and Asia. Most of their vaccination program had disastrous results, causing the very illness (polio, for example in India) and sterilizing young women (Kenya, with modified tetanus vaccines). Many of the children died. Many of the programs were carried out with the backing of the WHO and – yes – the UN Agency responsible for the Protection of Children, UNICEF.

"Most of these vaccination campaigns were implemented without the informed-consent of the children, parents, guardians or teachers, nor with the informed-consent, or with forged consent, of the respective government authorities. In the aftermath, The Gates Foundation was sued by governments around the world, Kenya, India, the Philippines – and more.

"Bill Gates has a strange image of himself. He sees himself as The Messiah who saves the world through vaccination – and through population reduction.

"Around the time, when the 2010 Rockefeller Report was issued, with its even more infamous 'Lock Step' Scenario, precisely the scenario of which we are living the beginning right now, Bill Gates talked on a TED show in California, "Innovating to Zero" about the use of energy.

"He used this TED presentation to promote his vaccination programs, literally saying, **"If we are doing a real good job vaccinating children, we can reduce the world population by 10% to 15%"**. (Emphasis added by the author.) Has this Satanic aim ever been mentioned to you before?

One further little known point about Gates, and which may explain his constant presence in this crisis: He has requested to be part of the Executive Board of the WHO, which means that he, an individual, now has the same authority to act as if he were a member state.

59. And then there is this very interesting point: What is being injected <u>is not a vaccine.</u>

Dr Trozzi from Ontario says the definition of a vaccine is "A preparation of a weakened or killed pathogen, such as a bacterium or virus, or of a portion of the pathogen's structure that upon administration to an individual stimulates antibody production or cellular immunity against the pathogen but is incapable of causing severe infection." -The American Heritage® Dictionary of the English Language, 5th Edition.

"So, vaccine means an injection or swallowed dose of a weakened, dead, or fragmented bacteria, virus or other infective organism, which you are trying to immunize against. Though the injection is dead, or too weak to cause significant illness, it does present the immune system with some of the parasite's surface markings, also called "antigens". This allows your body to prepare antibody and cellular defences against the parasite, so if in the future, you encounter it, your immune system will kill it quickly without you getting ill. That's great 150 year old science credited to its founder Louis Pasteur.

"Now: Please refer to page 11 on either of the Covid "vaccine" EAU briefings (Moderna ; Pfizer) to find in section 4.1 Vaccine Composition: "The vaccine contains a nucleoside-modified messenger RNA (modRNA) encoding the viral spike glycoprotein (S) of SARS-CoV-2." or "The vaccine contains a synthetic messenger ribonucleic acid (mRNA) encoding the pre-fusion stabilized spike glycoprotein (S) of SARS-CoV-2 virus."

"Hence, these new injections are Covid-19 genetic material. They are a modified part of the Covid-19 virus's genetic code, advertised to enter your cells, engage with and use your ribosomes which normally produce only your own cell's complex parts or "proteins" based on your genetic code and your messenger RNA. Naturally, inside your cells, your messenger RNAs bring your many natural proteins' designs from their hard copy within your DNA, to your cells' ribosomes outside of the nucleus. Hence your messenger RNA normally carry elements of your genetic code from your DNA that is within your cells' nuclei, to your ribosomes, which read the codes and produce your cellular machinery called "proteins". However, when the ribosomes are engaged by the viral messenger RNA injection, your cells start producing part of the virus: the viral "spike glycoprotein of SARS-CoV-2". So this is where it starts to have some relationship to vaccines, but it's very different. Here, your own cells have viral genes inside, directing them to spend nutrients and energy to produce and pump out copies of part of the Covid-19 virus into your circulation. The optimistic sales pitch here is that you end up with some parts of the Covid - 19 virus floating around in your body to hopefully stimulate a healthy immune response. On the other hand this highly experimental viral gene injection carries unknown risks and serious concerns."

Is it not extraordinary that this aspect of the vaccine has not been mentioned on the mainstream media?

60. I know of many doctors who have said that these vaccines are being launched in such a way that the human race is being treated as guinea pigs. The names of these doctors and the concerns that they raise can be found summarised in Appendix Two. Can they all be wrong?

61. In case what you have just read has not explained the facts about the Covid "vaccine" clearly enough, here is a slightly different explanation from Dr Carrie Madej. These are notes that were taken while watching her being interviewed:

In a normal vaccine you are given a small dose of the illness that your body fights and defeats and thus your body builds up an immunity.

The Covid vaccine is nothing like this: The manufacturers have taken a genetic code (RNA which does not occur naturally) and implanted it in a human body so that body manufactures the virus, which it then fights and, one hopes, destroys. But this is an entirely experimental procedure. It should have taken ten years of testing before being released. They have turned human beings into guinea pigs and have no idea if it is safe.

The Covid vaccine is covered in an envelope that prevents it being destroyed. More than this, the code can collect and transmit information wirelessly between the body and artificial intelligence.

When the new RNA technology was tried on ferrets and mice, the initial results were satisfactory but, after a while, the bodies of the vaccinated animals started to attack themselves and so they died. As a result of this, the US Supreme Court ruled that these trials should not be tested on humans.

So why is such a vaccine being used on humans? And why with so very little testing?

62. Vaccine ineffectiveness. As we say elsewhere, how about this extraordinary admission in the National Health Service leaflet which the author was sent when being invited to a vaccination; an invitation that he did not accept, "We do not yet know whether it (having the vaccine) will prevent you from

catching or passing on the virus."* Having read that, is it any wonder that a large number of people is refusing to be vaccinated?

Indeed, here is a case in point: One purpose of a vaccine is to encourage the production of antibodies and yet Win Dewsbury wrote to *The Daily Telegraph* on 21ˢᵗ April 2021 to say that, having had the vaccination in early February, she was tested over two months later only to discover that she had no antibodies. So, in spite of being vaccinated, apparently she has no protection against the virus. What was the point of being vaccinated?

*On page 11 of their and Public Health England's pamphlet, *Covid-19 Vaccination – A Guide for Older Adults.*

63.   And then how about "informed consent."? Proper medical practice involves the patient having all aspects of their proposed treatment explained to them individually. The author knows of nobody to whom such information has been offered, and therefore of nobody who has given their informed consent. Is this not extraordinary medical malpractice on a world-wide scale, especially when the populace has been conned by the propaganda in the media to flock (queuing in their hoards) to their local injection centres to be given a "jab"?

64.   And how about the people who have either suffered or died shortly after taking the vaccine? The deaths of boxer Marvellous Marvin Haggler and the nurse Tiffany Dover, both shortly after being vaccinated, being cases in point, but there have been hundreds of others.

65.   In February 2021, the UK Medical Freedom Alliance wrote to both Matt Hancock, the UK Secretary of State for Health and Care, and Nadhim Zahawi, Minister for Covid-19 Vaccine Deployment, calling for an immediate, urgent and independent audit of deaths that have occurred since the beginning of the Covid-19 vaccine rollout. They cited the government's own statistics that weekly care home deaths tripled in the two weeks between 8ᵗʰ and 22ⁿᵈ January, at a time when there was a massive increase in the rate of vaccinations of care home residents. And they also cited how this development seemed to have occurred throughout the world.

Has anyone seen any publicity in the mainstream media about this, or whether this request has been heeded by the government?

66. The illogicality of vaccine passports:
First, not everybody *can be* vaccinated and, secondly, not everybody *wants* to be vaccinated.

Thirdly, and most importantly, (as we have just mentioned) even the NHS has admitted that being vaccinated neither guarantees that you will not catch Covid, nor that you will not pass it on.

So why ban those who have not been vaccinated from entry to events, means of transport, pubs etc? Those in (say) the pub who have been vaccinated, on the assumption that the vaccine really does protect them, need not fear anyone who has not been vaccinated. On the other hand, those who have not been vaccinated through choice are free to take the risk that they might catch Covid from anyone, whether in a pub or elsewhere. Is not the requirement that we all have vaccine passports simply another example of the government wanting to control us *even more*?

And it's not as if vaccines can take the credit for reducing Covid deaths. Take this graph of the seven-day rolling average of Covid deaths in the UK:

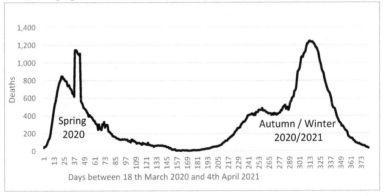

One cannot claim that the falling off of deaths since January 2021 has been due to the widespread vaccination programme when the very similar fall in deaths in the spring of 2020 happened long before any Covid vaccine had been invented, let alone distributed.

67. And then, for those who have been given the vaccine, has it resulted in any relaxing for them of the severe lockdown restrictions?

68. In February 2021, this letter was sent to Her Majesty Queen Elizabeth II by the author, after she had called those who refuse to take the vaccine "selfish."

"May it please Your Majesty,

With all due respect, I take exception to being called selfish for the reason that, at least for the present, I do not wish to take the Covid vaccination, and I take exception for the following reasons:

1. The NHS leaflet that I was sent inviting me to make an appointment says quite clearly "We do not yet know whether it (having the vaccine) will prevent you from catching or passing on the virus." Having read that, is it any wonder that I cannot see the point of taking the vaccine?
2. There has been insufficient time for this vaccine to be properly tested, and ...
3. ... nobody can possibly know, after so short a time, about any long-term effects that it might cause.
4. No informed consent has been mentioned or offered; an omission exacerbated by the BBC refusing to interview any professional who expresses doubts about the safety or efficacy of the vaccine.
5. I have heard of alarming cases, which were not reported in the media, in which numerous patients have died within a short period of time after receiving the vaccine. According to your government, over 240 people have already died shortly after receiving the vaccine. I am unsure which is more alarming: The deaths or the lack of reporting.

6. The drug companies that produce the vaccines have been given immunity from prosecution for the side-effects and worse that their vaccines might cause. I find this aspect both suspicious and very worrying.

I write this letter with all due respect and would suggest that you should consider my approach to this very important matter to be both common sense and prudent, and in no way selfish.

I remain Your Majesty's obedient servant,"

This letter was courteously acknowledged but, at the time of writing the six points remain unanswered.

Should not the accusation of selfishness by those refusing the vaccine have been withdrawn?

6   Other Concerns

6.a.   US / China Collaboration
69.   Why, under Dr Fauci's watch, did the US give $3.7 million to the Wuhan Laboratory in connection with CV-19, and yet the doctor has never owned up to this association?

6.b. The Silencing of the Sceptics
70.   With anti-Covid demonstrations being broken up by police with truncheons, is it not therefore likely that the channels of (currently) readily available information on what is really going on, will be shut down, thereafter making such vital information almost impossible to obtain?

71.   And then, while this book is being written, the government has introduced legislation entitled the Police, Crime, Sentencing and Courts Bill, that is intended to give the police new powers to control the length of protests, impose maximum noise levels and prosecute activists for causing "serious

annoyance", a concept that its opponents argue has not been clearly defined. Will any sort of anti-lockdown demonstration be savagely broken up, on the basis of the police deciding (nobody else but the police) that it's become a serious annoyance?

72. As has already been mentioned, even without this legislation, peaceful anti-lockdown demonstrations in London have been viciously broken up, and yet the Black Lives Matter and Extinction Rebellion demonstrations have been allowed to continue, despite the criminal damage that the demonstrators inflicted. Are we not justified in suspecting that such uneven-handedness shows that the Covid-sceptics are the government's enemy number one?

73. And this is not to mention the lack of reporting by the media of even the existence of the anti-lockdown demonstrations. Why are the authorities so determined to deprive those who are unhappy about what is going on of the oxygen of publicity?

74. With so much suppression of any alternative voice to what is happening, to the extent of calling those who protest "covid deniers", are we not entitled to think that something malevolent is going on?

6.c. The Silencing of the Professionals

75. It is clear that dissenting voices among professionals are no longer allowed. They, like us, have had their liberties removed. But, worse than that, too many doctors and scientists are happily taking the money to do what they are told to do and to neither question, nor show initiative and instead do what they know to be right.

Is this not utterly disgraceful? Especially when you remember that...

76. ... Doctors have all taken the Hippocratic oath which includes these promises:
"First and foremost I will be caring for my patients, taking care of their health and reducing their suffering."
"I will inform my patients correctly."

"Even under pressure, I will not use my medical knowledge for practice against humanity."
Does it not seem as if many doctors are breaking this oath because the "First do no harm" maxim is being undermined by the current treatments that they are being forced to offer?

77. It seems that our only hope is if doctors and nurses start to stand up for the truth. As is said elsewhere, various medical professionals have gone public with their grave concerns, decrying what is happening, speaking out against what they are being forced to do with some resigning in disgust. These people usually add that their colleagues are afraid of speaking out in case they lose their jobs.

Why do so many highly trained medical professionals, instead of standing up for the truth, simply " go with flow" and do what they know to be wrong?

6.d What about the 5G rays?

78. What the experts say is that, unlike its predecessors, 5G aims a very narrow beam of radio waves at your cell phone and therefore at you. The beams from 5G masts alters the cell membrane's permeability allowing toxic calcium ions to pass into cells. This causes sperm and testicular damage, neurological effects, cell death as well as cardiac and blood pressure problems.

How this works is it damages haemoglobin. Normally haemoglobin removes CO_2 from your organs, takes it to your lungs which you then breathe out. The haemoglobin collects oxygen from the lungs and takes it back to the organs. But it can only do this if it has the right amino acids, especially including histidine.

5G waves are thought to change the voltage of the calcium ions, thus making them toxic and driving them into the haemoglobin, damaging the amino acid structure so that it can no longer carry O_2. And so it would seem that CV-19 patients who die might well be suffering from either the man-manipulated CV virus, or exposure to 5G radio waves, or possibly both.

The problem is that, as in the case of vaccines, nobody is allowed to talk about this. Why on earth not?

(If you want more detail about the dangers of telephone wires and telephone signals generally, there is alarming proof provided by Arthur Firstenberg in *The Invisible Rainbow*. He points out that, ever since the first telephone cables were erected there has been a steady and definite incidence of heart disease, cancer, diabetes and obesity. It is an enthralling, if horrifying, read.)

6.e. What about the deaths in care homes at the start of the so-called pandemic?

79. Why were hospitals cleared of patients (who were moved to old people's homes without testing and where thousands of them died) leaving hospital wards empty (deliberately closed) with the result that, as we say below, over 33,000 people died from cancer and other non-Covid ailments through receiving no treatment?

80. When it was decided that hospitals should be emptied of patients, who were sent to care homes, why were blanket "Do not resuscitate" orders imposed on care home residents?

81. And why too were blanket "Do not attempt cardio-pulmonary resuscitation" orders also imposed?

82. In view of the last three points, are we not looking at wholescale criminal professional neglect?

6.f. Apparently empty hospitals

83. Why has at least one person, a brave lady, who filmed the main hospital in Gloucester being empty at the height of the second wave, been arrested for making this point public and severely criticised by the local MP, instead of having her amazing story properly answered by those in authority?

84. In the case of the above point, I happened to pass the press article about the above story to a neighbour, a doctor, asking him what he should make of it.

At the time of writing (three months later) the doctor has neither answered this question nor even spoken to me. One asks, therefore, "Is one no longer allowed even to ask questions?" It would seem not.

And I can personally confirm that hospitals have been emptied (effectively closed) because I attended a medical appointment in a local hospital on 1212th March 2020 (just before the first lockdown) and the consultant told me that, within a few days, the whole hospital would be emptied of patients. I was stunned by that announcement and realised that we were all entering new territory. So why is the fact of closed hospital wards never commented upon? And, indeed, when it is, why is the commentator castigated for pointing it out?

85. We have mentioned the lack of treatment (total lack of treatment) in hospitals for patients who were not suffering from Covid. At the time of writing and as has just been said (but it is staggering figure and needs to be repeated), over *33,000 excess deaths* have occurred as a result of deciding not to offer treatment to such patients. In other words, 33,000 people have died as a result of this decision. Why has nobody been held to account for such a truly terrible decision?

6.g. Covid Immunity

86. What about Covid immunity? I understand that our T cells, for example, may give us a natural immunity. There are various estimates but let us take the lowest which is that 30% of us are likely to have immunity to Covid, which means we can neither have it nor pass it on. Why have such people still been locked down?

6.h. The problems with Covid testing

87. The UK government uses the PCR test which stands for Polymerase Chain Reaction. What the government never tells you is that it is a highly unreliable test that was never designed for this purpose. Fortunately, in this case, the Portuguese government have realised that it is not reliable.

According to Off-Guardian, November 20, 2020, "An appeals court in Portugal has ruled that the PCR process is not a reliable test for Sars-Cov-2, and therefore any *enforced quarantine based on those test results is unlawful.*

"Further, the ruling suggested that any forced quarantine applied to healthy people could be a violation of their fundamental right to liberty.

"Most importantly, the judges ruled that *a single positive PCR test cannot be used as an effective diagnosis of infection.*

"The specifics of the case concern four tourists entering the country from Germany – all of whom are anonymous in the transcript of the case – who were quarantined by the regional health authority. Of the four, only one had tested positive for the virus, whilst the other three were deemed simply of "high infection risk" based on proximity to the positive individual. All four had, in the previous 72 hours, tested negative for the virus before departing from Germany.

"In their ruling, judges Margarida Ramos de Almeida and Ana Paramés referred to several scientific studies. Most notably this study by Jaafar et al., which found that – when running PCR tests with 35 cycles or more – the accuracy dropped to 3%, meaning up to 97% of positive results could be false positives."

"The ruling goes on to conclude that, based on the science they read, any PCR test using over 25 cycles is totally unreliable. Governments and private labs have been very tight-lipped about the exact number of cycles they run when PCR testing, but it is known to sometimes be as high as 45. Even fearmonger-in-chief Anthony Fauci has publicly stated anything over 35 is totally unusable."

And yet, if you go to the UK government's website, you will see that the free test they offer is this PCR test.

The UK government have paid no attention at all to what the Portuguese authorities have declared. Is that not a disgrace?

88.   The UK government also uses the Lateral Flow Test, which gives a faster result when testing for Covid-19. However, according to a recent study by the University of Oxford and Public Health England's Porton Down laboratory, the LFT being used in the pilot scheme across Liverpool succeeded in detecting Covid-19 in only 79.2 per cent of cases even when performed by laboratory staff.

When used by trained health professionals in the community, the detection rate fell to 73 per cent and when used by self-trained members of the public it fell to just 58 per cent. On top of that were the false positives: 0.32 per cent of people given the tests were falsely told they had the virus.

Should we put any faith in the Covid testing, especially when, according to the *Daily Telegraph* on 3rd April 2021, "Every report into the £37 billion test and trace system has concluded that it has been a massive waste of money."?

6.i. Transhumanism

89.   While not competent to go into this matter in any detail, if you turn to Appendix Two and the Glossary you will find there brief references to transhumanism and the worry, nay assertion, that the vaccine, by altering our DNA, will turn us into something that is no longer truly naturally human. Such a frightening thought should be the subject of an entirely separate book but, nonetheless, is this not an extremely worrying development?

6.j. The Great Reset – Is history repeating itself?

"The Great Reset" is the term, now in common parlance, like "Build Back Better", that is being used by the UK Government, the WHO, The World Economic Forum, and the likes of Bill Gates and Anthony Fauci, in which to frame the world's reorganisation as it recovers from the Covid crisis. There is no secret but the <u>Re</u>-set is very much underway. To put it briefly, the Re-set means that the world's population is to be strictly controlled by our leaders – as if this has not happened ever since the first lockdown in the spring of 2020.

The very word "<u>Re</u>-<u>set</u>" reminds the author of the Reformation, or <u>Re</u>-<u>formation</u> and as he has looked into both process of "<u>Re</u>-<u>organisation</u>", some striking parallels immediately emerge.

While here is not the place to consider all of the parallels, let us look at just a few:

90. The Reformation in England (in the mid sixteenth century) was led by a larger than life leader, King Henry VIII, who once stoutly professed one belief and then abandoned it to impose another, doing so with great and sustained cruelty. The Reset is being promoted in the UK by a larger than life politician, Boris Johnson, who used to promote extremely liberal attitudes but has now turned his government into a dictatorship that imposes severe curtailments of individual freedom. Is history repeating itself?

91. Amongst the general public, King Henry swept aside all opposition, bullying his parliament into agreeing with his criminal proposals. Johnson has done the same by emasculating Members of Parliament, with very few of them objecting, and how he has also allowed the police brutally to attack peaceful anti-lockdown demonstrations, imposing swingeing fines on the organisers. Is that not another interesting parallel?

92. In other words, most people at the time of the Reformation felt so overwhelmed by what was happening they meekly went along with the changes. So too, now, most people meekly wear their masks, keep six feet apart and just put up with the changes. Again, is this similarity not curious?

In one fell swoop:

93. King Henry destroyed the religious life of the country. Under Boris Johnson we have seen the bishops close all churches for public worship. Is there not a parallel here?

94. King Henry also destroyed the education system; Boris Johnson, too, has closed the schools. Again, is this not also a curious parallel?

95. King Henry destroyed the then "National Health Service", which the monasteries had provided, and which was not to be replaced for five hundred years. Boris Johnson has shut down the National Health Service to all but the 6% of people who have suffered from Covid. Once more, is this not an interesting parallel?

96. Likewise, by his actions, King Henry effectively destroyed the whole economic life of the country, not to mention closing down its welfare state which, like the monasteries' national health service, had also been provided by the monastic system. Hasn't Boris Johnson done exactly the same, not only borrowing £251 billion to pay for covid in 2020/21, but additionally forcing the bankruptcy of thousands of business, increasing the number of unemployed from 1.4 million to 1.7 million*, not to mention severely (may I use the word) "clobbering" the charitable sector.

*These figures are not the true figures because it excludes 6.8 million who were expected to be on Furlough at the end of March 2021. So that is 8.5 million currently not in work, compared to 1.4 million before this pandemic started. Why did we then, and why have we now, just stood by and let these disastrous events unfold?

97. And finally in this set of parallels, in England, at the time of the Reformation, a system was put in place whereby there could be no return to the past. Today, we are constantly being told that, despite the arrival of the vaccines, which one would have thought would lead to life returning to normal, the Great Reset will ensure that we endure a "New Normal" with no possibility of returning to the ways things used to be. Henry VIII is considered by many to have been a tyrant; might we not say the same of Boris Johnson?

6.k. The likely effect of the Great Reset

98.   If we take just some of the above points, namely the destruction of:

- Religious life
- Education
- A proper functioning health service
- A broken economy
- And a myriad of other disasters.

Are we not likely to find that these disasters are blamed on Covid (a disease that has affected just 6% of the population and killed as few as 1 in 500) and not on the politicians and disreputable scientists who made the woeful decisions?

99.   In other words, is not the UK population likely to be frightened by, and misled, by the proliferation of false propaganda into doing *anything* to avoid these disasters happening again and meekly accepting any restrictions to our liberty in such a cause?

100. One or more of the means that the government will use to impose the ever-growing number of restrictions is likely to be through the diktats of the UK Health Security Agency, which was launched on 1st April 2021. One of its apparent purposes is to vaccinate everyone against diseases before they materialise. (Thinks: How can one vaccinate against a disease if the disease doesn't even exist?)

Another, possibly more sinister, purpose is to "influence behaviour". Does this mean that we will be permanently subjected to an unending stream of propaganda in the media and, at the same time, suffering further restrictions on our already gravely depleted freedoms?

Might we be forgiven for thinking, if one looks at the graph of Covid deaths on page 23, where it can be clearly seen that the reduction in deaths has nothing to do with the roll out of vaccines, that nonetheless, those of us who refuse to be vaccinated will be falsely accused and blamed for fostering any on-going incidences of Covid cases?

6.l.   And finally, a question to sum up

101.   Although this is clearly a very nasty disease for those who catch it, at the time of writing, it has affected just 6.5% of the population and claimed the lives of less than 0.2%.

In other words, it has affected only a tiny proportion of the population – tiny – especially since 97% of the people who have caught Covid have recovered.

And so, since in the preface to this book I have suggested that the best way to decide whether the actions that someone has taken are good or not, we should apply the God-given maxim of "By their fruits ye shall know them", let us recap on some of the fruits that have been considered in this book:

1.   Covid is no chance occurrence. It was clearly anticipated. Q.1.
2.   It has been engineered by scientists. Q4.
3.   It is not highly contagious. Q12.
4.   It has affected only 1 in 500 in the UK. Q.15.
5.   The deaths from Covid have been significantly overstated. Q17.
6.   97% of those who have caught it have recovered. Q.25.
7.   The results from tests for Covid are seriously inaccurate. Q22 and Q88.
8.   The reporting of this disease has been, and still is, nothing but propaganda. Q.23.
9.   Doctors have been silenced for speaking out. Q24.
10. Using ventilators has made Covid patients suffer needlessly. Q. 33
11. Lockdowns, rather than improving the situation, have increased the deaths. Q.34.
12. Masks don't work. Q.39.
13. Masks make wearers more ill. Q.38
14. Protesters have been prevented from demonstrating. Q44.
15. Social distancing has also been deleterious to health. Q.45
16. Attendance at public worship has been forbidden. Q 47.
17. The vaccines have not been properly tested. Q.68.

18. The vaccines are not normal vaccines. Q.61.
19. The vaccines are ineffective. Q62.
20. Those who have been vaccinated have not been given back their freedoms. Q.67.
21. The drug companies that produce the vaccines have been given immunity from prosecution. Q.55.
22. Hospital wards have been closed. Q83.
23. There have been 33,000 extra deaths of people who have been denied treatment for non-Covid complaints. Q.85.
24. Doctors are refusing to speak out for fear of reprisals. Q.75.
25. The young have suffered most dreadfully. Q.38.
26. The government refuses to listen to any alternative point of view. Q.22
27. The incalculable damage lockdown has done to our economy with eight million out of work or on furlough. Q.96.
28. The vastly increased debts that this country now owes. Q.96
29. The pusillanimity of our politicians who have done so little (nothing) to hold the government to account. Q.91.
30. The UK government has behaved like a dictatorship, and a communist dictatorship at that. Q.90.

Are these not all simply terrible fruits? In short, and as others have said, doesn't the whole thing stink? Indeed, when we consider the above "fruits", are we not entitled to judge that "An enemy hath done this", and indeed an enemy, our government, that is not only shamefacedly still doing it but also doing nothing to change direction, and all the while refusing us permission to either talk about it, or demonstrate against it?

Let's finish with:

A Message of Hope
Many believe that the Devil is behind the Covid crisis. One thing I have learned from experience is that the Devil, while he is a bully, he is also an inveterate coward. This means that, if one stands up to him and tells others what he is doing, he will collapse into a pathetic heap of defeated ineffectiveness. One may be destroyed in the process but, by doing this, and with the aid of prayer, one can greatly diminish his influence.

Appendices:

Appendix One:
The Concerns of Polish Doctors – as published in *Christian Order* Volume 62 No.1.

This is a summary of the "Deep Concerns" that these doctors have raised and published originally in November 2020. Some of these points have already been covered in the main text but the author believes that it might be helpful to have these important points presented in this simple way:

1. After the initial panic over Covid-19 the objective facts now show a completely different picture from what was expected – there is no longer any medical and scientific justification for continuing with the restrictions.
2. The current crisis management has become completely disproportionate to the threat and is doing more harm than good.
3. We believe that mandatory measures have been introduced that do not have a scientific basis and that ...
4. ... A coronapanic has been created in the media ...
5. ... Without the possibility of an open debate
6. The strict repressive policy on coronavirus infections with minimum contact with other people, and little exercise allowed, prevents all people strengthening their immune system through a healthy lifestyle.
7. The initial estimated mortality from SARS-Cov 2 infection was largely *unconfirmed* in *any* country.
8. Covid is not a killer virus but an easy-to-treat disease.
9. The RT-PCR test is not useful for detecting and diagnosing a viral infection as it is intended only for research procedures. It gives many false positives.
10. If someone has tested positive, it does not mean they are clinically infected or sick or will be sick. So-called asymptomatic carriers do not infect others.

11.Most people already have innate or acquired immunity to influenza, coronavirus or other viruses. This is confirmed by the findings on the Diamond Princess cruise ship. Most of the passengers were elderly and ideally exposed to the transmission of the virus. However 75% were found to be not infected. So even in high-risk groups, most people are immune to the virus.

12.In the event of a risk of infection, you should strengthen your natural immunity through healthy nutrition, breathing fresh air, without a mask, reducing stress and satisfying social and emotional contacts.

13.Physical activity reduces depression and anxiety and improves energy levels, wellbeing and the overall quality of life.

14.The national health service has been paralyzed. Closed care clinics, reduced numbers of admission to hospitals, undiagnosed diseases requiring urgent treatment, untreated chronic diseases. All of these have added further to human suffering.

15.The spread of the virus occurs through droplet infection (only in patients who cough or sneeze) and aerosol spray in enclosed unventilated rooms. Therefore contamination is impossible in open air. Healthy people are almost incapable of transmitting this virus, hence they are not a threat to each other.

16.Also the transmission of the virus by objects (e.g., money, shopping or shopping carts) has not been scientifically proven.

17.It is clear that dissenting voices among professionals are no longer allowed. They, like everyone else, have had their liberties removed.

18.But, worse than that, too many doctors and scientists are happily taking the money to do what they are told to do and to neither question nor show initiative and do what they know to be right. They seem to have forgotten that…

19.… Doctors have all taken the Hippocratic oath which includes these promises:
"First and foremost I will be caring for my patients, taking care of their health and reducing their suffering."
"I will inform my patients correctly."

"Even under pressure, I will not use my medical knowledge for practice against humanity."

It would appear that many doctors are breaking this oath because the "First do no harm" maxim is being undermined by the current measures.

20. In the case of masks, the weave of the fibres in the cotton masks is of the order of micrometres, whereas the size of the virus is one thousand times smaller. So there are no physical grounds to claim that masks protect against airborne viruses.

21. Oxygen deficiency which is caused by masks occurs fairly quickly and has an effect similar to altitude sickness; which results in headache, nausea, fatigue, loss of concentration etc.,

    1. Patients also complain of sinus and breathing problems.
    2. Accumulated CO_2 leads to toxic acidification of the body, which adversely affects immunity.
    3. A room or workplace should contain no more than the standard 900 parts per million of CO_2, with a maximum of 1,200 in certain circumstances; but after wearing a mask for a minute this toxic limit is significantly elevated to three to four times these limits. It is like breathing in a poorly ventilated room.

22. Influenza vaccine studies show that in ten years only three vaccines have been developed that are more than 50% effective. Vaccinating the elderly does not seem to be effective. After the age of 75 the effectiveness is almost non existent.

23. Due to the constant mutation of viruses new vaccines are required each time.

24. The exemption from liability for the vaccine companies raises serious doubts.

25. In recent months, newspapers, radio and television have seemed to stand almost uncritically on the side of the authorities when the press (if it is a free press) should be critical and prevent one-sided government communication.

26. The doctors who wish to present what they believe to be the true picture, and the real dangers, are also surprised by the fact that many

videos and articles by numerous independent authorities and scientific experts are removed from social media. This situation is unacceptable in a free democratic country.

27. When presenting Covid statistics, there is no comparison of the current mortality with that of recent years.

28. The doctors regret the role played by the WHO calling for those with views that deviate from officially accepted opinion to be silenced by unprecedented media censorship.

29. Covid is not a killer virus but an easily treatable disease with a mortality rate comparable to that of seasonal flu.

30. Why do health advisers meet behind closed doors keeping independent experts and scientists out of public discussion, as well as preventing elected politicians from challenging government ministers with the questions that need asking?

Appendix Two –
What The Experts say about Covid-19 and, above all, the Vaccine.

These are notes taken from the video posted on:
http://www.thetruthseeker.co.uk/?p=222603
This video lasts about 30 minutes. It was released in December 2020.

	Contributor	What he or she said...
1	Andrew Kaufman – Medical doctor and forensic psychiatrist in the USA. Also Covileaks UK	1. This is not a real medical pandemic. 2. There has not been enough time to test any vaccine to prove it either safe or effective. 3. There has not been any definition of a new disease for it to be tested against. 4. There has not been a virus that has been identified to be the cause of this illness. 5. There is no need for a vaccine.
2	Hilde De Smet. Medical doctor from Belgium	1. Vaccine is not safe. 2. There is no global medical pandemic. 3. For twenty years the pharmaceutical industry has been trying to develop corona vaccines. They have never managed because they saw in the animal trials that there were serious side effects. 4. The pharmaceutical industry have been given the excuse to skip the animal trials in the case of this disease. Thus we humans are the guinea pigs and we might get severe side effects if we are exposed to new viruses.
3	Dr Nils R Fosse medical doctor from Norway	1. The vaccine has not been proven safe and effective. 2. It is new technology. 3. The death rates are not higher than during an average year. 4. Do your own research.
4	Dr Elizabeth Evans retired doctor	1. The covid vaccines are not proven. They are experimental vaccines. 2. There is only limited short-term safety data. 3. There is no evidence that this vaccine will prevent transmission of the virus. 4. There is no long-term safety data that these vaccines will not see the patient developing auto immune diseases , infertility and cancers later in life.

Appendix Two

	Contributor	What he or she said…
5	Dr Vernon Coleman	1. Doctors are not allowed to question the efficacy of this vaccine. 2. This is a pandemic that never was and a vaccine that was never needed. 3. The Covid-19 scam is the greatest hoax in history. 4. The principal of informed consent is essential in medicine. Patients are not being informed. They are denied information. 5. Watch brandnewtube for uncensored videos.
6	Professor Dolores Cahill. Molecular Biologist and immunologist in Ireland	1. The coronavirus is not as severe as was supposed. 2. We can treat the symptoms with vitamins D, C and E. 3. The lockdown, social distancing and masks were not necessary. 4. Which means the vaccine is also not necessary
7	Dr Zac Cox Holistic dentist and homeopath from the UK. Founder member of the world doctors alliance	1. There is no long term safety data on any of the vaccines. 2. They are experimenting on us which is against the Nuremburg code
8	Dr Anna Forbes UK medical doctor member of the UK medical freedom alliance	1. An over estimation of the public health risk. 2. The data has been misrepresented. 3. There is no informed medical consent.
9	Dr Ralph E R Sundbery medical doctor from Sweden	1. The Polymerase Chain Reaction (PCR) test is inaccurate. There have been so many false positives
10	Dr Daniel Cullum. Chiropractic physician from Turpen Oklahoma, USA	1. This is not a pandemic. The vaccine has not been proven safe or effective and I will not be taking it. There is no safe vaccine.
11	Dr Tom Cowan. Medical doctor from the USA	1. Health does not come from the injection of toxins into our bodies but from what it means to be human and pursuing that with all of your heart.
12	Kate Shemirani. Natural nurse from the UK	1. There is no pandemic. 2. The covid virus has never been proven to exist. 3. With so little safety testing this vaccine should not be taken. The government should be arrested for genocide

	Contributor	What he or she said...
13	Dr Johan Denis medical doctor and homeopath from Belgium	1. The vaccine is not proven safe or effective. 2. This is a fake pandemic. The coronavirus in terms of harmfulness, mortality and transmissibility is comparable to a seasonal flu. 3. He rejects the disproportionate measures that have been taken by governments and says that this has all been orchestrated to make you fearful enough to take the vaccine. 4. The vaccine has not been proven safe. It has been developed too quickly. 5. We have no idea what the long term affects will be. 6. There is no hurry nor emergency. 7. The vaccine might possibly change your DNA. It is irreversible and irreparable for all future generations. 8. It is an experiment on humanity. I will never give it to myself or my patients. 9. There is nanotechnology present in this vaccine. Nanobots in hydrogels have been developed for military purposes. 10. There are strong indications that it could make you a controllable puppet by means of your smart phone connected with the 5G network. In this way you could lose everything that makes you human. 11. See website of Robert Kennedy. Children's Health defence.org
14	Moritz Van der Borch Medical journalist from Germany	1. Do not take this vaccine. It is dangerous. 2. The pandemic is a fraud
15	Dr Anne Fierlafijn Medical doctor from Belgium	1. The vaccine has not been proven safe nor effective. 2. It is unacceptable that the companies that have produced it will incur no liability. 3. How can they expect doctors to inject it without doubt of doing harm? 4. The measures so far taken have caused far more damage than the virus itself. 5. Now is the time to stand up for your children and against the restrictions to your freedoms.

	Contributor	What he or she said...
16	Dr Kevin P Corbett, retired nurse and health scientist	1. The covid vaccines have not been proven safe or effective. 2. This is not a real medical epidemic. 3. The vaccines use synthetic products which may produce dangerous chemical reactions. 4. The vaccinations should be immediately stopped. 5. The vaccinations have been promoted through fear to maximise profit. 6. Standard precautions which normally protect the public have been disregarded due to ignorance, fear and profit. 7. The NHS should never be using it.
17	Dr Carrie Madej, Medical doctor from the USA. She has run two different clinics as well as being attendant physician training medical students for nineteen years.	1. There is no world wide pandemic. 2. The PCR tests were never developed or intended for detecting any infection. 3. Why are doctors being given financial incentives to diagnose covid-19? 4. There are copious instances of false positives being reported. 5. She will not take the vaccine nor recommend its use. 6. The human race is being injected with modified / synthetic RNA and DNA. 7. This is the first time it has ever been launched on the human race and with so little testing. 8. It is also being suggested that nano lipid technology be used. 9. There are awful things that could happen to us and it needs much more research before we go forward.
18	Dr Barrie Lando. Physician from the USA.	1. He has spent much of his time dealing with vaccine-damaged children and highly cautions anyone against taking the covid vaccine.
19	Sandy Lunoe Pharmacist from Norway	1. The vaccines are not proven safe or effective. 2. The vaccine can make the patient worse when he or she is infected with the disease. 3. In the UK the Medicines and Healthcare Profits Regulatory Agency has made an urgent request for an artificial intelligence software tool to process the high volume of expected adverse reactions to the vaccine

	Contributor	What he or she said...
20	Boris Dragin Licensed acupuncturist from Sweden	1. With forty years experience with complimentary medicine, he declares that this is not a real pandemic. 2. This is an assault on our human rights, our freedoms and our society. 3. You have to be mad to accept an untested experimental vaccine from a criminal manufacturer that ignores safety procedures in pursuit of enormous profits and especially where people are pressured into taking it. 4. No insurance company has agreed to insure against side effects after taking the vaccine. 5. The companies that produce the vaccine are immune from prosecution. 6. Let our leaders take it first.
21	Dr Piotr Rubas medical doctor from Poland	1. Strongly recommends against taking the vaccine. 2. There should be clinical trials lasting at least five years.
22	Dr Natalis Prego Cancelo medical doctor Spain	1. The vaccine is neither safe nor effective
23	Dr Rashid Buttar. Medical doctor from the USA	1. Stand up and fight against this, especially for your children
24	Dr Nour De San, medical doctor from France	1. It is not the principle of the vaccine. The problem is how they have got us to believe that it might be possible to produce a vaccine within a year, against a new disease and on a very, very large scale. 2. And to plan to vaccinate everyone on earth. 3. Anyone who has worked with vaccines knows that it takes a great deal of time to collect the data to ensure its efficacy and safety, and properly understand the long term effects.
25	Dr Kelly Brogan. Medical doctor in the USA	1. It was very hard to hear what she was saying but she mentioned a transhumanist agenda. 2. Vaccination is the penetration of the body mind and spirit by the state.
26	Dr Margaret Griesz-Brisson. Neurologist from Germany	1. What is happening to a defenceless population is both unethical, immoral and illegal. There needs to be both informed consent and clinical evidence of harmlessness beyond.

	Contributor	What he or she said...
27	Dr Sherri Tenpenny medical doctor from the USA	1. You have no recourse if this vaccine harms you. 2. The tests that were done on animals for the SARS resulted in the antibodies accelerating the infections making the patient much worse. 3. It is terrible to think of allowing pieces of the virus to enter the cell and be incorporated into the DNA of the recipient of that vaccine (transduction) 4. This is irreversible and permanently deforms your cells
28	Senta Depuydt Journalist from Belgium	1. The vaccines are an experimental product. 2. The risks are unknown and could have irreversible consequences. 3. Our politicians have agreed to let the vaccine producers enjoy immunity from prosecution and also to remove the need of risk evaluation, on the basis of no scientific reports, no debate and no amendments. She was talking of the EU Parliament but the same applies in the UK. The European Court of Justice in Luxembourg has been asked to cancel this immunity. 4. Our politicians have put blind faith into a dangerous experiment
29	Dr Heiko Santelmann medical doctor from Germany with forty years experience and ten years research on vaccines	1. He shouts out that this is not a real medical pandemic. 2. The vaccine has not been proven to be safe or effective. 3. He agrees with the British Medical Journal that the testing has not been done honestly. 4. If you study the results of the tests it is not 90% but only 0.2% effective. 5. Why does Gates spend billions promoting a vaccine that can sterilise men and women and even their unborn children
30	Dr Mikael Nordfors. Medical doctor from Sweden	1. There is no pandemic and 2. ...To give untested vaccine to the whole of humanity is madness and must be stopped now. 3. It is even worse to give it to children who do not suffer from Covid-19. 4. There will never be a vaccine as safe and effective as Vitamin D

	Contributor	What he or she said ...
31	Dr Elke F de Klerk a medical doctor from the Netherlands	1. This vaccine could sterilise girls. 2. It could lead to a deterioration in health and it could change your genetic blueprint / your genetic code

Appendix Three

Transcript of **Dr Reiner Fuellmich**'s video talk entitled:

Crimes Against Humanity

(First delivered in early 2021. Dr Fuellmich's emphases have been included.)

Hello. I am Reiner Fuellmich and I have been admitted to the Bar in Germany and in California for 26 years. I have been practising law primarily as a trial lawyer against fraudulent corporations such as Deutsche Bank, formerly one of the world's largest and most respected banks, today one of the most toxic criminal organizations in the world; VW, one of the world's largest and most respected car manufacturers, today notorious for its giant diesel fraud; and Kuehne and Nagel, the world's largest shipping company. We're suing them in a multi-million-dollar bribery case.

I'm also one of four members of the German Corona Investigative Committee. Since July 10, 2020, this Committee has been listening to a large number of international scientists' and experts' testimony to find answers to questions about the corona crisis, which more and more people worldwide are asking. All the above-mentioned cases of corruption and fraud committed by the German corporations pale in comparison in view of the extent of the damage that the corona crisis has caused and continues to cause.

This corona crisis, according to all we know today, must be renamed a "Corona Scandal" and those responsible for it must be criminally prosecuted and sued for civil damages. On a political level, everything must be done to make sure that no one will ever again be in a position of such power as to be able to defraud humanity or to attempt to manipulate us with their corrupt agendas. And for this reason, I will now explain to you how and where an international network of lawyers will argue this biggest tort case ever, the corona fraud scandal, which has meanwhile unfolded into probably the greatest crime against humanity ever committed.

Crimes against humanity were first defined in connection with the Nuremberg trials after World War II, that is, when they dealt with the main war criminals of the Third Reich. Crimes against humanity are today regulated in section 7 of the International Criminal Code. The three major questions to be answered in the context of a judicial approach to the corona scandal are:

1. Is there a corona pandemic or is there only a PCR-test pandemic? Specifically, does a positive PCR-test result mean that the person tested is infected with Covid-19, or does it mean absolutely nothing in connection with the Covid-19 infection?
2. Do the so-called anti-corona measures, such as the lockdown, mandatory face masks, social distancing, and quarantine regulations, serve to protect the world's population from corona, or do these measures serve only to make people panic so that they believe – without asking any questions – that their lives are in danger, so that in the end the pharmaceutical and tech industries can generate huge profits from the sale of PCR tests, antigen and antibody tests and vaccines, as well as the harvesting of our genetic fingerprints?
3. Is it true that the German government was massively lobbied, more so than any other country, by the chief protagonists of this so-called corona pandemic, Mr. Drosten, virologist at charity hospital in Berlin; Mr. Wieler, veterinarian and head of the German equivalent of the CDC, the Robert Koch Institute or RKI; and Mr. Tedros, Head of the World Health Organization or WHO; because Germany is known as a particularly disciplined country and was therefore to become a role model for the rest of the world for its strict and, of course, successful adherence to the corona measures?

Answers to these three questions are urgently needed because the allegedly new and highly dangerous coronavirus has not caused any excess mortality anywhere in the world, and certainly not here in Germany. But the anti-corona measures, whose only basis are the PCR-test results, which are in turn all based on the German Drosten test, have, in the meantime, caused the loss of innumerable human lives and have destroyed the economic existence of countless companies and individuals worldwide. In Australia, for example, people are thrown into prison if they do not wear a mask or do not wear it properly, as deemed by the authorities. In the Philippines, people who do not wear a mask or do not wear it properly, in this sense, are getting shot in the head.

Let me first give you a summary of the facts as they present themselves today. The most important thing in a lawsuit is to establish the facts – that is, to find out what actually happened. That is because the application of the law always depends on the facts at issue. If I want to prosecute someone for fraud, I cannot do that by presenting the facts of a car accident. So, what happened here regarding the alleged corona pandemic?

The facts laid out below are, to a large extent, the result of the work of the Corona Investigative Committee. This Committee was founded on July 10, 2020 by four lawyers in order to determine, through hearing expert testimony of international scientists and other experts:
1. How dangerous is the virus really?
2. What is the significance of a positive PCR test?
3. What collateral damage has been caused by the corona measures, both with respect to the world population's health, and with respect to the world's economy?

Let me start with a little bit of background information. What happened in May 2019 and then in early 2020? And what happened 12 years earlier with the swine flu, which many of you may have forgotten about? In May 2019, the stronger of the two parties which govern Germany in a grand coalition, the CDU, held a Congress on Global Health, apparently at the instigation of important players from the pharmaceutical industry and the tech industry. At this Congress, the usual suspects, you might say, gave their speeches. Angela Merkel was there, and the German Secretary of Health, Jens Spahn. But, some other people, whom one would not necessarily expect to be present at such a gathering, were also there: Professor Drosten, virologist from the Charite hospital in Berlin; Professor Wieler, veterinarian and Head of the RKI, the German equivalent of the CDC; as well as Mr. Tedros, philosopher and Head of the World Health Organization (WHO). They all gave speeches there. Also present and giving speeches were the chief lobbyists of the world's two largest health funds, namely the Bill and Melinda Gates Foundation and the Wellcome Trust. Less than a year later, these very people called the shots in the proclamation of the worldwide corona pandemic, made sure that mass PCR tests were used to prove mass infections with Covid-19 all over the world, and are now pushing for vaccines to be invented and sold worldwide.

These infections, or rather the positive test results that the PCR tests delivered, in turn became the justification for worldwide lockdowns, social distancing and mandatory face masks. It is important to note at this point that the definition of a pandemic was changed 12 years earlier. Until then, a pandemic was considered to be a disease that spread worldwide, and which led to many serious illnesses and deaths. Suddenly, and for reasons never explained, it was supposed to be a worldwide disease only. Many serious illnesses and many deaths were not required any more to announce a pandemic. Due to this change, the WHO, which is closely intertwined with the global pharmaceutical industry, was able to declare the swine flu pandemic in 2009, with the result that vaccines were produced and sold worldwide on the basis of contracts that have been kept secret until today. These vaccines proved to be completely unnecessary because the swine flu eventually turned out to be a mild flu, and never became the horrific plague that the pharmaceutical industry and its affiliated universities kept announcing it would turn into, with millions of deaths certain to happen if people didn't get vaccinated. These vaccines also led to serious health problems. About 700 children in Europe fell incurably ill with narcolepsy and are now forever severely disabled. The vaccines bought with millions of taxpayers' money had to be destroyed with even more taxpayers' money. Already then, during the swine flu, the German virologist Drosten was one of those who stirred up panic in the population, repeating over and over again that the swine flu would claim many hundreds of thousands, even millions of deaths all over the world. In the end, it was mainly thanks to Dr. Wolfgang Wodarg and his efforts as a member of the German Bundestag, and also a member of the Council of Europe, that this hoax was brought to an end before it would lead to even more serious consequences.

Fast forward to March of 2020, when the German Bundestag announced an Epidemic Situation of National Importance, which is the German equivalent of a pandemic in March of 2020 and, based on this, the lockdown with the suspension of all essential constitutional rights for an unforeseeable time, there was only one single opinion on which the Federal Government in Germany based its decision. In an outrageous violation of the universally accepted principle "audiatur et altera pars", which means that one must also hear the other side, the only person they listened to was Mr. Drosten.

That is the very person whose horrific, panic-inducing prognoses had proved to be catastrophically false 12 years earlier. We know this because a whistleblower named David Sieber, a member of the Green Party, told us about it. He did so first on August 29, 2020 in Berlin, in the context of an event at which Robert F. Kennedy, Jr. also took part, and at which both men gave speeches. And he did so afterwards in one of the sessions of our Corona Committee.

The reason he did this is that he had become increasingly sceptical about the official narrative propagated by politicians and the mainstream media. He had therefore undertaken an effort to find out about other scientists' opinions and had found them on the Internet. There, he realized that there were a number of highly renowned scientists who held a completely different opinion, which contradicted the horrific prognoses of Mr. Drosten. They assumed – and still do assume – that there was no disease that went beyond the gravity of the seasonal flu, that the population had already acquired cross- or T-cell immunity against this allegedly new virus, and that there was therefore no reason for any special measures, and certainly not for vaccinations.

These scientists include **Professor John Ioannidis** of Stanford University in California, a specialist in statistics and epidemiology, as well as public health, and at the same time the most quoted scientist in the world; **Professor Michael Levitt**, Nobel prize-winner for chemistry and also a biophysicist at Stanford University; the German professors **Kary Mölling, Sucharit Bhakti, Klud Wittkowski**, as well as **Stefan Homburg**; and now many, many more scientists and doctors worldwide, including Dr. Mike Yeadon. Dr. Mike Yeadon is the former Vice-President and Scientific Director of Pfizer, one of the largest pharmaceutical companies in the world. I will talk some more about him a little later.

At the end of March, beginning of April of 2020, Mr. Sieber turned to the leadership of his Green Party with the knowledge he had accumulated, and suggested that they present these other scientific opinions to the public and explain that, contrary to Mr. Drosten's doomsday prophecies, there was no reason for the public to panic. Incidentally, Lord Sumption, who served as a judge at the British supreme court from 2012 to 2018, had done the very same thing at the very same time and had come to the very same conclusion: that there was no factual basis for panic and no legal basis for the corona measures. Likewise, the former President of the German federal constitutional court expressed – albeit more cautiously – serious doubts that the corona measures were constitutional. But instead of taking note of these other opinions and discussing them with David Sieber, the Green Party leadership declared that Mr. Drosten's panic messages were good enough for the Green Party. Remember, they're not a member of the ruling coalition; they're the opposition. Still, that was enough for them, just as it had been good enough for the Federal Government as a basis for its lockdown decision, they said. Then subsequently, the Green Party leadership called David Sieber a conspiracy theorist, without ever having considered the content of his information, and then stripped him of his mandates. Now let's take a look at the current actual situation regarding the virus's danger, the complete uselessness of PCR tests for the detection of infections, and the lockdowns based on non-existent infections. In the meantime, we know that the health care systems were never in danger of becoming overwhelmed by Covid-19. On the contrary, many hospitals remain empty to this day and some are now facing bankruptcy. The hospital ship Comfort, which anchored in New York at the time, and could have accommodated a thousand patients, never accommodated more than some 20 patients. Nowhere was there any excess mortality. Studies carried out by Professor Ioannidis and others have shown that the mortality of corona is equivalent to that of the seasonal flu. Even the pictures from Bergamo and New York that were used to demonstrate to the world that panic was in order proved to be deliberately misleading.

Then, the so-called "Panic Paper" was leaked, which was written by the German Department of the Interior. Its classified content shows beyond a shadow of a doubt that, in fact, the population was deliberately driven to panic by politicians and mainstream media. The accompanying irresponsible statements of the Head of the RKI – remember the [German] CDC – Mr. Wieler, who repeatedly and excitedly announced that the corona measures must be followed unconditionally by the population without them asking any question, shows that that he followed the script verbatim. In his public statements, he kept announcing that the situation was very grave and threatening, although the figures compiled by his own Institute proved the exact opposite.

Among other things, the "Panic Paper" calls for children to be made to feel responsible – and I quote –"for the painful tortured death of their parents and grandparents if they do not follow the corona rules", that is, if they do not wash their hands constantly and don't stay away from their grandparents. A word of clarification: in Bergamo, the vast majority of deaths, 94% to be exact, turned out to be the result not of Covid-19, but rather the consequence of the government deciding to transfer sick patients, sick with probably the cold or seasonal flu, from hospitals to nursing homes in order to make room at the hospitals for all the Covid patients, who ultimately never arrived. There, at the nursing homes, they then infected old people with a severely weakened immune system, usually as a result of pre-existing medical conditions. In addition, a flu vaccination, which had previously been administered, had further weakened the immune systems of the people in the nursing homes. In New York, only some, but by far not all hospitals were overwhelmed. Many people, most of whom were again elderly and had serious pre-existing medical conditions, and most of whom, had it not been for the panic-mongering, would have just stayed at home to recover, raced to the hospitals. There, many of them fell victim to healthcare-associated infections (or nosocomial infections) on the one hand, and incidents of malpractice on the other hand, for example, by being put on a respirator rather than receiving oxygen through an oxygen mask. Again, to clarify: Covid-19, this is the current state of affairs, is a dangerous disease, just like the seasonal flu is a dangerous disease. And of course, Covid-19, just like the seasonal flu, may sometimes take a severe clinical course and will sometimes kill patients. However, as autopsies have shown, which were carried out in Germany in particular, by the forensic scientist Professor Klaus Püschel in Hamburg, the fatalities he examined had almost all been caused by serious pre-existing conditions, and almost all of the people who had died had died at a very old age, just like in Italy, meaning they had lived beyond their average life expectancy.

In this context, the following should also be mentioned: the German RKI – that is, again the equivalent of the CDC – had initially, strangely enough, recommended that no autopsies be performed. And there are numerous credible reports that doctors and hospitals worldwide had been paid money for declaring a deceased person a victim of Covid-19 rather than writing down the true cause of death on the death certificate, for example a heart attack or a gunshot wound. Without the autopsies, we would never know that the overwhelming majority of the alleged Covid-19 victims had died of completely different diseases, but not of Covid-19. The assertion that the lockdown was necessary because there were so many different infections with SARS-COV-2, and because the healthcare systems would be overwhelmed is wrong for three reasons, as we have learned from the hearings we conducted with the Corona Committee, and from other data that has become available in the meantime: A. The lockdown was imposed when the virus was already retreating. By the time the lockdown was imposed, the alleged infection rates were already dropping again. B. There's already protection from the virus because of cross- or T-cell immunity. Apart from the above mentioned lockdown being imposed when the infection rates were already dropping, there is also cross- or T-cell immunity in the general population against the corona viruses contained in every flu or influenza wave. This is true, even if this time around, a slightly different strain of the coronavirus was at work. And that is because the body's own immune system remembers every virus it has ever battled in the past, and from this experience, it also recognizes a supposedly new, but still similar, strain of the virus from the corona family. Incidentally, that's how the PCR test for the detection of an infection was invented by now infamous Professor Drosten.

At the beginning of January of 2020, based on this very basic knowledge, Mr. Drosten developed his PCR test, which supposedly detects an infection with SARS-COV-2, without ever having seen the real Wuhan virus from China, only having learned from social media reports that there was something going on in Wuhan, he started tinkering on his computer with what would become his corona PCR test. For this, he used an old SARS virus, hoping it would be sufficiently similar to the allegedly new strain of the coronavirus found in Wuhan. Then, he sent the result of his computer tinkering to China to determine whether the victims of the alleged new coronavirus tested positive. They did.

And that was enough for the World Health Organization to sound the pandemic alarm and to recommend the worldwide use of the Drosten PCR test for the detection of infections with the virus now called SARS-COV-2. Drosten's opinion and advice was – this must be emphasized once again – the only source for the German government when it announced the lockdown as well as the rules for social distancing and the mandatory wearing of masks. And – this must also be emphasized once again – Germany apparently became the centre of especially massive lobbying by the pharmaceutical and tech industry because the world, with reference to the allegedly disciplined Germans, should do as the Germans do in order to survive the pandemic. C. And this is the most important part of our fact-finding: the PCR test is being used on the basis of false statements, NOT based on scientific facts with respect to infections. In the meantime, we have learned that these PCR tests, contrary to the assertions of Messrs. Drosten, Wieler and the WHO, do NOT give any indication of an infection with any virus, let alone an infection with SARS-COV-2. Not only are PCR tests expressly not approved for diagnostic purposes, as is correctly noted on leaflets coming with these tests, and as the inventor of the PCR test, Kary Mullis, has repeatedly emphasized. Instead, they're simply incapable of diagnosing any disease. That is: contrary to the assertions of Drosten, Wieler and the WHO, which they have been making since the proclamation of the pandemic, a positive PCR-test result does not mean that an infection is present. If someone tests positive, it does NOT mean that they're infected with anything, let alone with the contagious SARS-COV-2 virus. Even the United States CDC, even this institution agrees with this, and I quote directly from page 38 of one of its publications on the coronavirus and the PCR tests, dated July 13, 2020.

First bullet point says: "Detection of viral RNA may not indicate the presence of infectious virus or that 2019 nCOV [novel coronavirus] is the causative agent for clinical symptoms."

Second bullet point says: "The performance of this test has not been established for monitoring treatment of 2019 nCOV infection."

Third bullet point says: "This test cannot rule out diseases caused by other bacterial or viral pathogens."

It is still not clear whether there has ever been a scientifically correct isolation of the Wuhan virus, so that nobody knows exactly what we're looking for when we test, especially since this virus, just like the flu viruses, mutates quickly. **The PCR swabs take one or two sequences of a molecule that are invisible to the human eye and therefore need to be amplified in many cycles to make it visible.**

Everything over 35 cycles is – as reported by the New York Times and others – considered completely unreliable and scientifically unjustifiable. However, **the Drosten test, as well as the WHO-recommended tests that followed his example, are set to 45 cycles.** Can that be because of the desire to produce as many positive results as possible and thereby provide the basis for the false assumption that a large number of infections have been detected?

The test cannot distinguish inactive and reproductive matter. **That means that a positive result may happen because the test detects, for example, a piece of**

debris, a fragment of a molecule, which may signal nothing else than that the immune system of the person tested won a battle with a common cold in the past. Even Drosten himself declared in an interview with a German business magazine in 2014, at that time concerning the alleged detection of an infection with the MERS virus, allegedly with the help of the PCR test, that these PCR tests are so highly sensitive that even very healthy and non-infectious people may test positive. At that time, he also became very much aware of the powerful role of a panic and fear-mongering media, as you'll see at the end of the following quote. He said then, in this interview: "If, for example, such a pathogen scurries over the nasal mucosa of a nurse for a day or so without her getting sick or noticing anything, then she's suddenly a MERS case. This could also explain the explosion of case numbers in Saudi Arabia. In addition, the media there have made this into an incredible sensation."

Has he forgotten this? Or is he deliberately concealing this in the corona context because corona is a very lucrative business opportunity for the pharmaceutical industry as a whole? And for Mr. Alford Lund, his co-author in many studies and also a PCR-test producer. In my view, it is completely implausible that he forgot in 2020 what he knew about the PCR tests and told the business magazine in 2014. In short, this test cannot detect any infection, contrary to all false claims stating that it can. An infection, a so-called "hot" infection, requires that the virus, or rather a fragment of a molecule which may be a virus, is not just found somewhere, for example, in the throat of a person without causing any damage – that would be a "cold" infection. Rather, a "hot" infection requires that the virus penetrates into the cells, replicates there and causes symptoms such as headaches or a sore throat. Only then is a person really infected in the sense of a "hot" infection, because only then is a person contagious, that is, able to infect others. Until then, it is completely harmless for both the host and all other people that the host comes into contact with. **Once again, this means that positive test results, contrary to all other claims by Drosten, Wieler, or the WHO,** mean nothing with respect to infections, as even the CDC knows, as quoted above.

Meanwhile, a number of highly respected scientists worldwide assume that there has never been a corona pandemic, but only **a PCR-test pandemic**. This is the conclusion reached by many German scientists, such as professors Bhakti, Reiss, Mölling, Hockertz, Walach and many others, including the above-mentioned Professor John Ioannidis, and the Nobel laureate, Professor Michael Levitt from Stanford University.

The most recent such opinion is that of the aforementioned **Dr. Mike Yeadon**, a former Vice-President and Chief Science Officer at Pfizer, who held this position for 16 years. He and his co-authors, all well-known scientists, published a scientific paper in September of 2020 and he wrote a corresponding magazine article on September 20, 2020. Among other things, he and they state – and I quote: "We're basing our government policy, our economic policy, and the policy of restricting fundamental rights, presumably on completely wrong data and assumptions about the coronavirus. If it weren't for the test results that are constantly reported in the media, the pandemic would be over because nothing really happened. Of course, there are some serious individual cases of illness, but there are also some in every flu epidemic. There was a real wave of disease in March and April, but since then, everything has gone back to normal. Only the positive results rise and sink wildly again and again, depending on how many tests are carried out. But the real cases of illnesses are over. There can be no talk of a second wave. The allegedly new strain of the coronavirus is ..."– Dr. Yeadon continues – "... only new in that it is a new type of the long-known corona virus. There are at least four coronaviruses that are endemic and cause some of the common colds we experience, especially in winter. They all have a striking sequence similarity to the coronavirus, and because the human immune system recognizes the similarity to the virus that has now allegedly been newly discovered, a T-cell immunity has long existed in this respect. 30 per cent of the population had this before the allegedly new virus even appeared. Therefore, it is sufficient for the so-called herd immunity that 15 to 25 per cent of the population are infected with the allegedly new coronavirus to stop the further spread of the virus. And this has long been the case." Regarding the all-important PCR tests, Yeadon writes, in a piece called "Lies, Damned Lies and Health Statistics: The Deadly Danger of False Positives", dated

September 20, 2020, and I quote "The likelihood of an apparently positive case being a false positive is between 89 to 94 per cent, or near certainty."

Dr. Yeadon, in agreement with the professors of immunology, Kamera from Germany, Kappel from the Netherlands, and Cahill from Ireland, as well as the microbiologist Dr. Arve from Austria, all of whom testified before the German Corona Committee, explicitly points out that a positive test does not mean that an intact virus has been found.

The authors explain that what the PCR test actually measures is – and I quote: "Simply the presence of partial RNA sequences present in the intact virus, which could be a piece of dead virus, which cannot make the subject sick, and cannot be transmitted, and cannot make anyone else sick."

Because of the complete unsuitability of the test for the detection of infectious diseases – tested positive in goats, sheep, papayas and even chicken wings – Oxford Professor Carl Heneghan, Director of the Centre for Evidence-Based Medicine, writes that the Covid virus would never disappear if this test practice were to be continued, but would always be falsely detected in much of what is tested. Lockdowns, as Yeadon and his colleagues found out, do not work. Sweden, with its laissez-faire approach, and Great Britain, with its strict lockdown, for example, have completely comparable disease and mortality statistics. The same was found by US scientists concerning the different US states. It makes no difference to the incidence of disease whether a state implements a lockdown or not.

With regard to the now infamous Imperial College of London's Professor Neil Ferguson and his completely false computer models warning of millions of deaths, he says that – and I quote: "No serious scientist gives any validity to Ferguson's model." He points out with thinly veiled contempt – again I quote: "It's important that you know, most scientists don't accept that it ..." – that is, Ferguson's model – "was even faintly right. But the government is still wedded to the model." Ferguson predicted 40 thousand corona deaths in Sweden by May and 100 thousand by June, but it remained at 5,800 which, according to the

Swedish authorities, is equivalent to a mild flu. If the PCR tests had not been used as a diagnostic tool for corona infections, there would not be a pandemic and there would be no lockdowns, but everything would have been perceived as just a medium or light wave of influenza, these scientists conclude. Dr. Yeadon in his piece, "Lies, Damned Lies and Health Statistics: The Deadly Danger of False Positives, writes: "This test is fatally flawed and must immediately be withdrawn and never used again in this setting, unless shown to be fixed." And, towards the end of that article, "I have explained how a hopelessly performing diagnostic test has been, and continues to be used, not for diagnosis of disease, but it seems solely to create fear".

Now let's take a look at the current actual situation regarding the severe damage caused by the lockdowns and other measures. Another detailed paper, written by a German official in the Department of the Interior, who is responsible for risk assessment and the protection of the population against risks, was leaked recently. It is now called the "False Alarm" paper. This paper comes to the conclusion that there was that there was and is no sufficient evidence for serious health risks for the population as claimed by Drosten, Wieler and the WHO, but – the author says –there's very much evidence of the corona measures causing gigantic health and economic damage to the population, which he then describes in detail in this paper. This, he concludes, will lead to very high claims for damages, which the government will be held responsible for. This has now become reality, but the paper's author was suspended.

More and more scientists, but also lawyers, recognize that, as a result of the deliberate panic-mongering, and the corona measures enabled by this panic, democracy is in great danger of being replaced by fascist totalitarian models. As I already mentioned above, in Australia, people who do not wear the masks, which more and more studies show, are hazardous to health, or who allegedly do not wear them correctly, are arrested, handcuffed and thrown into jail. In the Philippines, they run the risk of getting shot, but even in Germany and in other previously civilized countries, children are taken away from their parents if they do not comply with quarantine regulations, distance regulations, and mask-wearing regulations. According to psychologists and psychotherapists who testified before the Corona Committee, children are traumatized en masse, with the worst psychological consequences yet to be expected in the medium and long-term. In Germany alone, bankruptcies are expected in the fall to strike small- and medium-sized businesses, which form the backbone of the economy. This will result in incalculable tax losses and incalculably high and long-term social security money transfers for –among other things – unemployment benefits.

Since, in the meantime, pretty much everybody is beginning to understand the full devastating impact of the completely unfounded corona measures, I will refrain from detailing this any further.

Let me now give you a summary of the legal consequences. The most difficult part of a lawyer's work is always to establish the true facts, not the application of the legal rules to these facts. Unfortunately, a German lawyer does not learn this at law school, but his Anglo-American counterparts do get the necessary training for this at their law schools. And probably for this reason, but also because of the much more pronounced independence of the Anglo-American judiciary, the Anglo-American law of evidence is much more effective in practice than the German one. A court of law can only decide a legal dispute correctly if it has previously determined the facts correctly, which is not possible without looking at all the evidence. And that's why the law of evidence is so important. On the basis of the facts summarized above, in particular those established with the help of the work of the German Corona Committee, the legal evaluation is actually simple. It is simple for all civilized legal systems, regardless of whether these legal systems are based on civil law, which follows the Roman law more closely, or whether they are based on Anglo-American common law, which is only loosely connected to Roman law.

Let's first take a look at the unconstitutionality of the measures. A number of German law professors, including professors Kingreen, Morswig, Jungbluth and Vosgerau have stated, either in written expert opinions or in interviews, in line with the serious doubts expressed by the former president of the federal constitutional court with respect to the constitutionality of the corona measures, that these measures – the corona measures – are without a sufficient factual basis, and also without a sufficient legal basis, and are therefore unconstitutional and must be repealed immediately. Very recently, a judge, Thorsten Schleif is his name, declared publicly that the German judiciary, just like the general public, has been so panic-stricken that it was no longer able to administer justice properly. He says that the courts of law – and I quote – "have all too quickly waved through coercive measures which, for millions of people all over Germany, represent massive suspensions of their constitutional rights. He points out that German citizens – again I quote – "are currently experiencing the most serious encroachment on their constitutional rights since the founding of the federal republic of Germany in 1949". In order to contain the corona pandemic, federal and state governments have intervened, he says, massively, and in part threatening the very existence of the country as it is guaranteed by the constitutional rights of the people.

What about fraud, intentional infliction of damage and crimes against humanity? Based on the rules of criminal law, **asserting false facts concerning the PCR tests or intentional misrepresentation**, as it was committed by Messrs. Drosten, Wieler , as well as the WHO, can only be assessed as fraud. Based on the rules of civil tort law, this translates into intentional infliction of damage. The German professor of civil law, Martin Schwab, supports this finding in public interviews. In a comprehensive legal opinion of around 180 pages, he has familiarized himself with the subject matter like no other legal scholar has done thus far and, in particular, has provided a detailed account of the complete failure of the mainstream media to report on the true facts of this so-called pandemic. Messrs. Drosten, Wieler and Tedros of the WHO all knew, based on their own expertise or the expertise of their institutions, that the PCR tests cannot provide any information about infections, but asserted over and over again to the general public that they can, with their counterparts all over the world repeating this. And they all knew and accepted that, on the basis of their recommendations, the governments of the world would decide on lockdowns, the rules for social distancing, and mandatory wearing of masks, the latter representing a very serious health hazard, as more and more independent studies and expert statements show. Under the rules of civil tort law, all those who have been harmed by these PCR-test-induced lockdowns are entitled to receive full compensation for their losses. In particular, there is a duty to compensate – that is, a duty to pay damages for the loss of profits suffered by companies and self-employed employed persons as a result of the lockdown and other measures.

In the meantime, however, the anti-corona measures have caused, and continue to cause, such devastating damage to the world population's health and economy that the crimes committed by Messrs. Drosten, Wieler and the WHO must be legally qualified as actual crimes against humanity, as defined in section 7 of the International Criminal Code. How can we do something? What can we do? Well, the class action is the best route to compensatory damages and to political consequences. The so-called class action lawsuit is based on English law and exists today in the USA and in Canada. It enables a court of law to allow a complaint for damages to be tried as a class action lawsuit at the request of a plaintiff if:

1. As a result of a damage-inducing event ...
2. A large number of people suffer the same type of damage.

Phrased differently, a judge can allow a class-action lawsuit to go forward if common questions of law and fact make up the vital component of the lawsuit. Here, the common questions of law and fact revolve around the worldwide PCR-test-based lockdowns and its consequences. Just like the VW diesel passenger cars were functioning products, but they were defective due to a so-called defeat device because they didn't comply with the emissions standards, so too the PCR tests –which are perfectly good products in other settings – are defective products when it comes to the diagnosis of infections. Now, if an American or Canadian company or an American or Canadian individual decides to sue these persons in the United States or Canada for damages, then the court called upon to resolve this dispute may, upon request, allow this complaint to be tried as a class action lawsuit. If this happens, all affected parties worldwide will be informed about this through publications in the mainstream media and will thus have the opportunity to join this class action within a certain period of time, to be determined by the court. It should be emphasized that nobody must join the class action, but every injured party can join the class.

The advantage of the class action is that only one trial is needed, namely, to try the complaint of a representative plaintiff who is affected in a manner typical of everyone else in the class. This is, firstly, cheaper, and secondly, faster than hundreds of thousands or more individual lawsuits.

And thirdly, it imposes less of a burden on the courts. Fourthly, as a rule it allows a much more precise examination of the accusations than would be possible in the context of hundreds of thousands, or more likely in this corona setting, even millions of individual lawsuits.

In particular, the well-established and proven Anglo-American law of evidence, with its pre-trial discovery, is applicable. This requires that all evidence relevant for the determination of the lawsuit is put on the table. In contrast to the typical situation in German lawsuits with structural imbalance, that is, lawsuits involving on the one hand a consumer, and on the other hand a powerful corporation, the withholding or even destruction of evidence is not without consequence; rather the party withholding or even destroying evidence loses the case under these evidence rules.

Here in Germany, a group of tort lawyers have banded together to help their clients with recovery of damages. They have provided all relevant information and forms for German plaintiffs to both estimate how much damage they have suffered and join the group or class of plaintiffs who will later join the class action when it goes forward either in Canada or the US. Initially, this group of lawyers had considered to also collect and manage the claims for damages of other, non-German plaintiffs, but this proved to be unmanageable.

However, through an international lawyers' network, which is growing larger by the day, the German group of attorneys provides to all of their colleagues in all other countries, free of charge, all relevant information, including expert opinions and testimonies of experts showing that the PCR tests cannot detect infections. And they also provide them with all relevant information as to how they can prepare and bundle the claims for damages of their clients so that, they too, can assert their clients' claims for damages, either in their home country's courts of law, or within the framework of the class action, as explained above.

These scandalous corona facts, gathered mostly by the Corona Committee and summarized above, are the very same facts that will soon be proven to be true either in one court of law, or in many courts of law all over the world.

These are the facts that will pull the masks off the faces of all those responsible for these crimes. To the politicians who believe those corrupt people, these facts are hereby offered as a lifeline that can help you readjust your course of action, and start the long overdue public scientific discussion, and not go down with those charlatans and criminals.

Appendix Four –

Not Forgetting Those who have Suffered as a Result of Covid-19

The main problem, if not criticism, that this book faces is, thus far, that it has not mentioned the undeniable fact that many people have suffered from covid. In other words, while this book has focused on the apparent malintent shown by our government in the way that it has handled the so-called pandemic, and it has done so with very sound reason, it has not referred to the appalling suffering that those with covid, as well as their nearest and dearest, have undergone.

Although this book has confined itself to asking questions, it should not overlook the fact that covid is a very nasty disease.

Let us, therefore, look briefly at the suffering:

> Those who have caught covid have endured agonising suffering.

> Those who have died have suffered agonising deaths, particularly those patients on ventilators.

> Those suffering from covid have also been separated from their family and friends. This denial of loving access, and the heart-break involved, has applied both to those in hospitals as well as in care homes.

> And then there has been the distress and suffering endured by the NHS and other medical staff who have treated covid patients.

The answer to these undeniable facts, and while it has not been mentioned in the press, is that many, many doctors have complained that most, if not all, of the above suffering, could have been avoided if they had been allowed to treat their patients in the way that they had been trained. Had the usual drugs been allowed there would have been fewer and shorter hospitalizations, and many fewer deaths.

Had normal routine coronavirus treatments been allowed, there would have been very few hospitalisations.

Had autopsies been allowed then many deaths reported as due to covid would have been corrected and reclassified appropriately.

This book ends not with yet another question but the statement of fact that the government created and exacerbated the appalling scenes that we have witnessed on our televisions by denying doctors and staff the use of proper anti-coronavirus medicines and procedures. Indeed, to all intents and purposes, this campaign looks like genocide; indeed it is hard to read Dr Reiner Fuellmich's talk (Appendix Three) and not come to this very conclusion.

It is the view of the author as well as some of those who have helped and encouraged the preparation of this book, that this campaign of denying effective treatment to hundreds of thousands of patients, has been planned deliberately to frighten us all so much that we have willingly accepted the need for such damaging lockdown regulations, the wearing of masks, the need for social distancing with days on end of miserable isolation, the threats of fines and prison sentences, not to mention needless periods of quarantine.

The answer to those who may regard this book as anti-covid propaganda is that it is not denying covid and it is not saying that it is not a very nasty disease; it is simply pointing out that the government has deliberately made the suffering far more extensive than it need have been.

Acknowledgements

Thank you, Michael Morley, for writing such an encouraging foreword and also for all your help with the text. Your diligence and support have been essential in terms of getting this book to market.

Thank you, Liz Phillips, for your encouragement and support, both early on during its preparation, not to overlook your suggestions and great help in spotting "typos". And your help has been particularly remarkable when I know that you have been so busy fighting against the iniquities of the Covid Crisis on a number of other fronts.

And thank you also, Brian King, for not only suggesting that St Edward's Press publish such a book but for so kindly encouraging me to publish it once it had been completed.

And thank you too, Daniel Joyce and Zenon Kuzik, for making sure I kept at it and, in Daniel's case, for your invaluable help with the script.

Glossary

Antibodies
: A protein used by the immune system to identify and neutralise foreign objects such as viruses.

Antigens
: Molecular structures on the outside of a pathogen the presence of which triggers an immune response. Vaccines are meant to encourage the production of antigens.

Contagion
: A disease which is spread by touching someone or something.

Coronavirus
: Coronaviruses are groups of related RNA viruses that can cause respiratory tract infections including the common cold, SARS, MERS and Covid-19.

Covid-19
: A disease caused by a new strain of coronavirus resulting in severe / acute infection of the respiratory system. CO stands for Corona. V stands for Virus. 19 is the year (2019) in which it was discovered.

Covid Lateral Flow Test
: A testing method for coronaviruses which detects about 75% of Covid cases.

Cycles Threshold
: See PCR Test

DNA
: Deoxyribose nucleic acid. It is a self-replicating material that is present in nearly all living organisms as the main constituent of chromosomes. It is the carrier of genetic information.

Epidemiologist
: Someone who studies patterns of health and disease.

Fraud
: A person or thing intended to deceive others.

Gates, Bill
: An American business magnate who co-founded Microsoft. He is reputed to be worth around £140bn (2021) and, with no medical qualifications, is spearheading the vaccination of the whole world with vaccines in which he has invested unfathomable sums. As is said in this book, (1) these vaccines are reckoned by many medical specialists around the world to be extremely dangerous, and (2) are likely to result in millions of deaths leading to a significant reduction in the world's population.

GAVI	Global Alliance for Vaccines and Immunisation. This was co-founded by Bill and Melinda Gates. Its aim is to vaccinate (in effect) the whole world with a view to protecting everyone against dangerous diseases. See also Immunity below. It is immune from any criminal investigation or prosecution.
Herd immunity	This is a form of indirect protection from infectious diseases that occurs when a sufficient percentage of the population has become immune to an infection. The WHO has recently changed the definition of herd immunity to imply that it results solely from the use of vaccines and no longer from self-acquired immunity.
Immunity	The capability of an organism to resist a particular infection by harmful microorganisms. It results from the action of specific antibodies or sensitised white blood cells. The WHO has recently changed the definition of herd immunity to imply that it results solely from the use of vaccines.
Immunologist	A medical doctor who specialises in treating allergies, asthma and other immune system disorders.
Infection	This occurs when another organism enters your body and causes a disease.
Incubation	The process or period of time in which harmful microorganisms are present in your body but do not (yet) produce the effects of the disease.
Lateral Flow Test	See Covid Lateral Flow Test.
Lymphocytes	Lymphocytes are a type of immune cell in the blood. An increase in lymphocytes is a sign of a viral infection.
MERS	Middle East Respiratory Syndrome. It is a coronavirus that was identified in Saudi Arabia in 2012.
Pandemic	A disease which is prevalent over a whole country or the world. Until about 2010, the definition of a pandemic included the expectation of many serious illnesses and deaths. This expectation has now been removed from the definition, thus justifying the treatment of covid-19 as if it were an emergency.
Pathogen	An organism that can produce a disease.

PCR Test	Polymerase Chain Reaction. The designer of this test, Kary Mullis deceased, never intended it for the purpose for which the government has used it during the Covid crisis. The test is reckoned to be about 90% inaccurate.

The problem with the accuracy of the PCR tests concerns RT-qPCR, which stands for Reverse Transcriptase–Quantitative Polymerase Chain Reaction and the cycle threshold that is used. During the test a fluorescence signal increases proportionally to the amount of amplified nucleic acid. If the fluorescence reaches a specified threshold within a certain number of PCR cycles (CT or cycle threshold value), the sample is considered a positive result.

To a layman this seems to imply that, to make the sample visible, you increase the magnification (cycle threshold). While the general view is that everything over 35 cycles is considered to be totally unreliable, the WHO recommends that the tests are set to 45 cycles.

Is it any surprise that the PCR tests are so inaccurate?

It should be noted that the WHO has issued a warning that the PCR tests do not work and yet most governments still promote their use.

PPE Equipment	Personal Protective Equipment.
R Number	Reproduction number. It relates to the average number of secondary infections by a single infected person. An R Number below one should mean that the incidence of the disease is declining.
RNA	Ribonucleic Acid. A nucleic acid present in all living cells. Its principal role is to act as a messenger carrying instructions from DNA for controlling the synthesis of proteins although in some viruses it is RNA, rather than DNA, that carries the genetic information.
RT-qPCR	See P C R Test.
SARS	Severe Acute Respiratory Syndrome. This is a respiratory disease caused by an associated coronavirus.

SARS Covid-2	This is the coronavirus found in 2019. SARS Cov-1 was discovered in about 2002.
T Cells	These are a type of lymphocyte. They are one of the most important white blood cells of the immune system, playing a central role in an immune response.
T Cell immunity	An immune response that does not involve antibodies.
Track and Trace	A plan whereby anyone who developed the symptoms of Covid-19 is tested and, if that is positive, all close recent contacts are told to self-isolate.
Transhumanism	The belief or theory that the human race can evolve beyond its current physical and mental limitations, especially by means of science and technology. Many people believe that the current anti-covid vaccinations are designed to achieve such evolution by injecting modified RNA into the human body; something the US Supreme Court decreed should not be done.
Vaccine	A substance used to stimulate the production of antibodies and thereby provide immunity against one or several diseases. It is prepared from the causative agent of the disease, its products or a synthetic substitute treated to act as an antigen without inducing the disease.
	Please note that at least two of the Covid vaccines do not fall under this definition. Instead, here is how they are officially described, "The vaccine contains a synthetic messenger ribonucleic acid (mRNA) encoding the pre-fusion stabilized spike glycoprotein (S) of SARS-CoV-2 virus." Hence, they are injections of genetic material, which is believed to have been obtained from aborted foetuses. They have not been prepared from the causative agent of the disease.
Virologist	Someone who studies viruses.
Virus	A sub-microscopic infectious agent that replicates only inside the cells of a living organism.
WHO	The World Health Organisation says that its purpose is to promote worldwide health, keep the world safe and protect the vulnerable.

Index